# CONSIDERING DIVORCE?

## CRITICAL THINGS YOU NEED TO KNOW

by

Melinda Eitzen, JD, Joanna Jadlow, CPA, CFP®, CDFA™

& Brenda Lee Roberts, M. Ed. LPC

**Considering Divorce?**
**Critical Things You Need To Know**

iUniverse books may be ordered through booksellers or by contacting:

iUniverse
1663 Liberty Drive
Bloomington, IN 47403
www.iuniverse.com
1-800-Authors (1-800-288-4677)

ISBN: 978-1-4917-0008-2 (sc)
ISBN: 978-1-4917-0009-9 (e)

Print information available on the last page.

iUniverse rev. date: 04/12/2019

# Table of Contents

# CHAPTER 1:

# MAKING THE DECISION

# TO DIVORCE

# Deciding to Divorce:  Not a Quick or Easy Decision

The decision to begin the divorce process can be frightening and the unknown overwhelming. In working with couples in divorce situations, it has been our experience that either one or both of them have known that the marriage was over for some time. The decision to follow through with the divorce is usually avoided for a multitude of reasons such as "staying in it for the children," "financially it's not a good time," "maybe they'll change" and/or "I'd rather be in a terrible marriage than be single again." Whatever the reason, people tend to stay too long. The idea in our society that people divorce rashly or on a whim has not been our experience. We see quite the opposite.

Sometimes, when a person has been in a marriage for a long time or has never been in a "good" romantic relationship, they become used to the situation and have trouble recognizing that this is not what marriage is supposed to be. A spouse may become accustomed to criticism, belittlement, screaming, being ignored, never knowing where their spouse is, infidelity, having little or no access to marital funds, and numerous other unhealthy behaviors. It can be very difficult to recognize the problems and address them.

Before moving forward with divorce, people often want to make sure that they are making the right decision. It is not uncommon for a Family Law attorney to refer their client to a marriage therapist or individual therapist prior to filing for divorce in order to help their client gain clarity as to whether or not to move forward with the divorce process.

# Marriage Counseling

Marriage counseling has the potential to help you avoid separation and divorce. It may help to relight the spark that went out, sometimes years ago. It can help improve communication, defuse anger, provide a new sense of hope, settle the panic, heal resentments, teach a new way of resolving conflict, renew trust, reduce conflict, increase intimacy, balance expectations, minimize defensiveness and teach you how to disagree without destroying the marriage. For those who truly haven't made up their mind, marriage counseling can provide the platform for a couple to reconnect, recover from an affair, redefine expectations, identify new dreams, rekindle old dreams, build/rebuild communication skills, and allow for concrete changes to be made.

However, just scheduling the appointment and going to counseling does not save your marriage. It requires time and the commitment to doing an extensive amount of emotional work. Going just for the sake of going will not work. Marriage counseling only helps couples who want to help themselves. Just one person going to counseling can affect the marital relationship, but it won't fix it. It takes both partners to work on the wholeness of their relationship.

*There are some issues that marriage counseling cannot fix.*

Honesty is imperative; it cannot work if both of you are not honest about your relationship histories and current marriage. There are many counselors who will not work with a couple if there is an active affair occurring. Marriage counseling cannot address addictions and the issues behind them. It cannot fix domestic violence problems. These are things that have to be addressed by participating in individual counseling and perhaps inpatient or outpatient treatment.

There are many people that do not begin marriage counseling until they have already decided to divorce. According to marriage and relationship expert, Dr. John Gottman,

> *"The average couple waits six years before seeking help for marital problems. Keeping in mind the fact that half of all marriages fail in the first seven years, the average couple lives for far too long with unhappiness."*

When people have already made up their minds to divorce before going to marriage counseling, they are often waiting for the opportunity or support that marriage counseling offers to deliver the message that they want to divorce or validation that it's Ok to want to divorce.

Counseling is rarely a quick fix. Deep seated issues and long standing habits of dysfunctional communication in your marriage cannot be fixed overnight. It is hard work. Very rarely are the problems all one person's fault; therefore, you both have to be willing to make changes. Sometimes additional work outside of marriage counseling may be needed, such as individual therapy.

**3**

# Individual Counseling / Therapy

There are times when only one person in the marriage decides to go to therapy, either because their significant other won't join them or because they need to see a therapist on their own to work through their questions about the marriage. Even when only one person in the marriage goes to therapy, it can affect the relationship. It has the potential to change the marriage positively or it may offer clarity to the individual on whether or not to stay in the marriage.

Individual therapy can also help with other issues that are impacting the marriage. It offers those with addictions the opportunity to find new ways of coping other than turning to alcohol, drugs, food, pornography or other destructive behaviors. It can provide support for victims of domestic violence. It may also be appropriate for batterers as it can help them work on anger management, stress relief and safe communication tools. For those needing additional support, therapists may also provide references to outside groups, such as addiction programs and batterer intervention programs.

# Key Point:
# You do have choices.

You can choose to stay in the relationship going forward without expectation of change, which means asking yourself,

> *"Can I stay in this relationship if it doesn't change?"*
>
> *"If things stay exactly the way they are right now,*
> *can I be happy in this relationship?"*

You can also choose to stay in the relationship with the expectation that it must change, which means asking yourself,

> *"Can I stay in this relationship if things improve within a certain period of time?"*
>
> *"How long am I willing to give this relationship a chance to work and to see if things really do change?"*

Your final choice might be, "I cannot stay in this relationship anymore. I have given it time to change and it has not. I have waited to see if it would work and it is not. I can no longer stay in this relationship."

## Alternatives to Counseling

If you find that counseling is not something you want to participate in because you do not like it or do not believe in it, there are other ways to help you gain clarity about your marriage.

## Pros and Cons

**One way is to make a list of pros and cons about the marriage. Ask yourself:**

- What are the good things about my marriage?
- In what areas of my marriage am I happy?
- What are the not so good things about my marriage?
- In what areas of my marriage am I unhappy?
- What are the things I would like to keep the same about my marriage?
- What are the things I would like to change about my marriage?

List as many things as you can, set it aside for a few hours or days, come back to it and see if there are any other things you can add.

# Example:

| Positive Things About My Marriage | Negative Things About My Marriage |
|---|---|
| We like to laugh | We fight almost daily |
| We enjoy going on spontaneous trips | I feel like my feelings and opinions don't matter |
| We have two beautiful children | His / her family knows too much personal stuff |
| We have great sex | I'm certain he / she is having an affair |
| We have a great home | We're not best friends anymore |

# What Needs to Change

**Another option is to make a list of what each of you would need to do to save the marriage.** Start by identifying what you know you need to work on first. What am I doing to contribute to the failure of this marriage? Work through a list of changes you know you need to make. Then, after you have looked at yourself, think about what you need your spouse to do or change in order for you to stay in the marriage.

## Example:

| How I Could Change | What I Need Him / Her to Do or Change |
|---|---|
| Let go of the small stuff | Not go out with co-workers so often |
| Be more spontaneous | Help with the children more |
| Not react negatively | Help with dinner/dishes |
| Talk about what is bothering me | Really listen when I am talking |
| Not share so much with his / her family | Show me love more often |

Be honest with yourself

and be as detailed as you need to be.

*Are the expectations that you have for yourself*
*and your spouse reasonable?*

*If the things you are wanting from your spouse*
*do not happen, are you willing to continue*
*in the relationship as it currently is?*

*How long will you stay in the relationship*
*if it does not change?*

# Mind Mapping

Another tool for working through decisions is called Mind Mapping. Mind Mapping can be a therapeutic, visual way of helping one make decisions based on every available thought about a specific situation.

Wikipedia defines Mind Mapping as:

> *"A mind map is a diagram used to represent words, ideas, tasks, or other items linked to and arranged around a central key word or idea. Mind maps are used to generate, visualize, structure, and classify ideas, and as an aid to studying and organizing information, solving problems, making decisions, and writing."*

The process of mind mapping when considering divorce might include writing the word "marriage" or "divorce" in the center of the page and then beginning to throw out all of your important thoughts about marriage or divorce such as "money", "children", "career", "where I would live", "how family views it", "religious beliefs", "sad", "disappointed", "afraid", "their anger" and then off of those topics start generating thoughts about each one. The goal is to exhaust your mind of ALL of the thoughts associated with each topic. Once you have finished, identify the things you can control by circling those items and identifying the things you can't control by marking through those items.

> *Once you have identified the things that you can control, begin looking at how you might solve or work through the items you believe you do have control over. The things you can't control are the items that should get the least amount of focus going forward.*

Circling those things that you have control over and marking through those things that you do not have control over may very well help you figure out if the issues are solvable, which can help lead you to the decision of whether or not to stay in the marriage. Should you come to the decision to no longer stay in the marriage, it is very important to be aware of what you will experience next.

# Picture of Mind Mapping

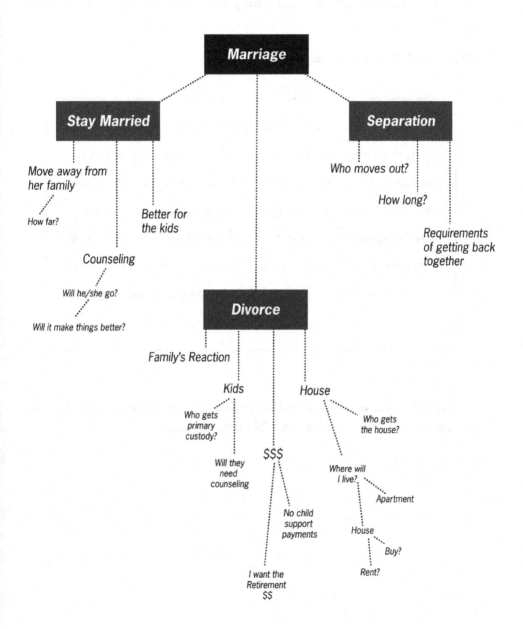

# Decision Tree

For those of you that have a more analytic mindset, another tool is called a Decision Tree.

Wikipedia defines a Decision Tree as:

*A decision tree is a decision support tool that uses a tree-like graph or model of decisions and their possible consequences, including chance event outcomes, resource costs, and utility. It is one way to display an algorithm. Decision trees are commonly used in operations research, specifically in decision analysis, to help identify a strategy most likely to reach a goal. Another use of decision trees is as a descriptive means for calculating conditional probabilities. "*

A Decision Tree is very similar to the process of Mind Mapping; however, it differs because it is a more structured, "if / then" process.

# Picture of Decision Tree

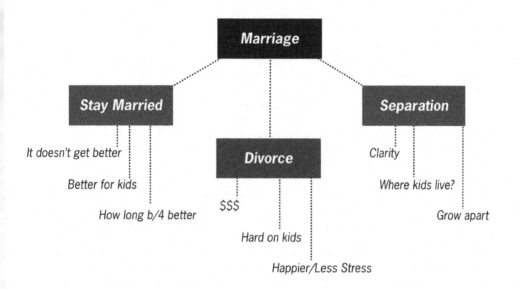

# CHAPTER 2:

# TELLING HIM

# OR HER

How you tell your spouse that you want a divorce

can significantly impact how the rest of your

divorce proceedings go.


You may be unhappy, sad, disappointed or angry;

however, don't let your emotions

get the best of you.

# Examples of how you can tell him / her:

1.      Verbally tell them privately at home.

2.      Tell them in front of a marriage counselor.

3.      Leave the already filed divorced papers in an envelope for them to find on the kitchen table.

4.      Have a process server show up at work or home and hand them the divorce papers (like on television when someone says "you've been served").

5.      Hire a moving van when they are out of town and move out half of the furniture.

**Later on in this chapter we will more fully discuss the pros/cons and impact of the five choices above.**

# Here is a list of tips
# for telling your spouse you want a divorce
### courtesy of Family Law Software, Inc.

There is a clear delineation in most divorces of "the leaver" and "the left." The leaver is usually in the stronger position psychologically and in his or her social circle. It seems silly and adolescent, but that's the way it works out. On the other hand, the left person feels wounded. The harder the "leave-taking" statement, the worse the wound. The worse the wound, the more likely to trigger "wounded-animal" type behaviors.

# Think carefully about how you want to do this.

- Prepare for all sorts of guilt to be laid on you (bad wife or husband, bad mother or father, bad person, cruel, selfish, etc.), and for verbal abuse. Be prepared to respond calmly. Know what you will say.
A few examples of what you can say may be:
"I can see how you might feel that way."
"I can hear your frustration. Maybe it is best if we talk again later."
"I'm ending this conversation for now. Things are too heated. Let's talk again in a half hour / in a couple of hours / later today / tomorrow."

- Avoid triggering your spouse's hot buttons.

- Prepare for promises to change. Be aware that people who are frightened, but unable to express that emotion, may channel it into anger directed at you, or into promises to change.

- It may make sense to prepare your spouse over time. Discuss divorce as a growing likelihood.

- Do not expect alcoholism or drug abuse to change, despite promises. There is an overwhelming body of evidence that once you say you are going to leave, your spouse's problems with alcohol or drug abuse will become even worse. Sometimes, they become temporarily better, but, without therapy or other interventions, they usually become worse fairly soon.

- Use "I" messages, not "you" messages. "I feel that I need to start a new life." "I feel that this marriage is not working for me." Do not say, "You never did your share. You were a lousy spouse." etc.

- Consider breaking this message in a public place with some privacy -- an uncrowded beach, street or restaurant. The public setting will encourage your spouse to respond in a restrained and rational fashion.

- Break the news during the daytime. Morning is best.

- Break the news when you are both sober and drug-free, if possible.

- Be confident. Walk firmly. Be physically as much at eye-level as possible. Speak calmly. Be prepared to drain yourself of anger before you begin and during the conversation if you feel it welling up. You can feel sorrow, yes. Anger, no.

- During the conversation, take deep breaths to relax.

- If you have children, assure your spouse that he or she is still father or mother to the children and that this is important to you. Bolster his or her esteem in any reasonable, honest way you can.

- Don't listen to abuse if you can avoid it. Say "I understand how you feel, but I do not think it helps either of us to have you go on this way" and leave or hang up.

- Don't get angry. Don't take the bait when he or she presses your hot buttons.

- Tell your spouse that you want to tell the children together, calmly, when you are both ready. This is important for the children.

- Often it is best, after the "I want a divorce" conversation, for immediate physical separation. You should have a place to go selected, even if you hope to remain in the home. You can go there if your spouse refuses to leave.

- If you fear a physical response, you may have to just leave, and perhaps not let your spouse know where you are.

Family Law Software Inc.
http://www.familylawsoftware.com/splitgen/sp/gn/tellingspouseyouwantadivorce.htm

The way you choose to tell your spouse will depend on your circumstances and will affect the tone of the case. If you are married to a decent non-violent person, you can most likely tell him/her privately at home or in front of a marriage counselor. If you are not afraid of your spouse and you do not fear he or she will try to harm you (or throw your clothes in the yard and burn them), then telling him/her at home or with a counselor will help to set **a tone of respect and allow the other person to receive the information without feeling defensive.**

If you are in individual therapy, practice or role-play with your therapist about how you will say the words to your spouse. Treat it like any other important, difficult family discussion.

> *In fact, we suggest that you have this conversation before you file for divorce. This decreases the negative surprise reaction. The more you can keep them informed of each step, the more respected your spouse will feel.*

By keeping your spouse fully informed of the steps you are taking, he/she is more likely to be reasonable when it comes to negotiating or determining the terms of the divorce. Having knowledge of what is going to happen at every step can provide a sense of security in a very uncertain time for both of you. It might be a good idea, regardless of how you choose to let your spouse know about the divorce, to let one close friend or relative know you are going to deliver the news to your spouse so that you will have someone to talk to afterward.

### What if you have a spouse who you think may react in a violent, extreme, unsafe, or "clothes burning in the yard" type way?

If you have NOT sought help before, now may be the time to do so. In this type of situation, telling them with a marriage counselor present might be an option if you can get them to go to the counselor. It may be better to choose to leave the already filed divorce papers in an envelope on the kitchen table for your spouse to find at a time when you will be safe and out of reach.

# There is also a good argument for having a process server serve them.

The reason this might be the best choice is because when the person is formally served by a process server (versus leaving in an envelope or handing it to him yourself), two things happen. First, the person is officially notified from the court's perspective and must answer within twenty days or things in the lawsuit could happen without him or her (these are Texas rules, other states may be different). The value to this is that it usually inspires your spouse to hire a lawyer quickly and the lawyer will usually help to keep the conflict down and advise the person against irrational behavior. (We are using the term "usually" because some lawyers behave in a way that increases the conflict). Secondly, having a process server deliver the paperwork to your spouse may be the preferred method because in many counties there is a standing order which applies to a person once they are formally served. It would not officially apply if they received it from you by hand or left in an envelope on the table.

The Dallas County standing order is included in **Appendix 6** to give you an idea of the typical contents.

If you are in a county that has a standing order, it may not keep your spouse from burning your clothes in the yard, but at least now he or she is violating a court order, which the judges take very seriously. For those who have abusive spouses, deciding to divorce your spouse is not easy and can be very frightening. There are many resources available to help you determine the best way to notify your spouse of the divorce and also help you (and your children) find temporary housing while you are going through the divorce.

**Appendix 5** is a list of organizations in the Dallas/Fort Worth area that specialize in domestic violence situations. Other counties across the country may have similar organizations. Check your local listings for domestic violence support services.

# Why It Matters How You Tell Them

## Why does it matter which method you choose for telling your spouse you want a divorce?

## Why should you be concerned about the tone you are setting for the case?

## Here is an example of why the tone matters:

Linda and Doug have been married 30 years. Doug wants a divorce. He does not view Linda as reasonable or rational. Linda goes out of town to move her mother into an assisted living facility four hours away by plane ride. While Linda is gone, and without telling her, Doug pulls up two moving vans and removes one-third of the furnishings from their home, including Linda's beloved pet, a Cockatoo. Linda comes home from her trip to discover what Doug has done and that he wants a divorce.

Fast forward to six months later. Doug, Linda and their lawyers are trying to negotiate a divorce settlement. Doug and Linda have spent a large amount of money on attorney's fees. They have spent three times more than they normally would have. The reason that they have spent three times more is because they had to have a temporary hearing in order for Linda to get the Cockatoo back.

Linda was furious during the entire divorce process about how the case started. She felt betrayed, tricked, and that Doug got the upper hand. This made it very difficult for her to see reasonable settlement offers as reasonable offers. She wanted financial recompense for what she viewed as Doug's bad behavior at the beginning of the case. Had Doug told her in advance that he wanted a divorce and talked to her about which items would make sense for him to remove from the house, they would have saved a lot of money, anxiety and heartache.

# How to Tell Them

Again, how you tell your spouse sets the tone for the entire case. First of all, it is important that the children not be around when this conversation takes place. Whether they are at daycare, school, a relative's house or with the babysitter, be sure that both of you will have uninterrupted time to discuss and process the information, away from the children. Ensure that you have time before and after the news has been shared to think through the conversation and the reactions.

It is important to remember that you have already gone through some, if not all, of the grief process. It is likely that your spouse has not even begun the grief process. The moment you tell them, they start the grief process. It is impossible to know for sure how they will react. There may be no emotion, a lot of emotion, a delayed emotional reaction or anywhere in between. What happens after you say you want a divorce is uncharted territory for both of you.

> *Communicate with your spouse about the divorce with facts,*
> *try to stay away from extreme emotions,*
> *and do what you can to stay calm.*

One way to start the conversation is to discuss what has not been working for you. What changes you had hoped to see in yourself that have not happened. What changes you had hoped to see in the relationship that have not happened. This is not the time to dredge up the past, bring up prior arguments, or remind them of prior hurts and/or disappointments. Keep it brief because he or she will not be able to hear a lengthy explanation or lots of details in that moment.

It is possible that your spouse will want to argue with you about this decision. If you are certain about moving forward with divorce, it is best to set a boundary by saying "I have made my decision" rather than engaging in an argument. If future conversations are needed, try to stick by the same guidelines as the initial conversation. These guidelines include setting aside time for the conversation, keeping the discussion brief, sticking to facts, and stopping the conversation if emotions run too high with a commitment to return to it when you have both calmed down.

# Affairs

There are many people who will choose to have an affair instead of having a conversation with their spouse about their unhappiness in the marriage and their desire to divorce. Many people may even begin having an affair before they come to terms with the fact that they are unhappy in their marriage and want a divorce. There is a quote by Dr. Phil that says:

> *"You don't ever solve a relationship problem by turning away*
>
> *from your partner."*

Having an affair does not do anything for your marriage and it keeps you from having the difficult conversations necessary to see if it can work.

Many people still have an affair though and do eventually get caught...sometimes intentionally. They forget the stories that they have used for cover-up or simply become careless about their actions, such as leaving their cell phones on the counter for their spouse to go through or leaving email accounts signed in on the computer. Many affairs happen with co-workers, neighbors or other parents they come across at school or extracurricular activities. In the cases of neighbors, school and/or extracurricular activities, it is more than likely that their children and your children know each other, participate in some of the same activities or sit in the same classrooms. Regardless of their affiliation, both families are impacted by the choice to have an affair and nobody's marriages are saved.

If it is not too late, we recommend waiting to have the new relationship until after you are divorced. Even though an affair is usually a symptom of a failed marriage, rather than the cause, it is still a very identifiable betrayal. The old saying "Hell has no fury like a woman scorned" also applies to men as well.

Affairs have a profound effect upon your divorce. An affair can greatly affect how the betrayed spouse portrays you to the children. It can cause irreparable damage to the relationship between you and your children. It usually also causes the betrayed spouse to demand more in the financial settlement. If you are currently married and having an affair, our advice is to stop the affair immediately. You can resume that relationship after the divorce is finalized.

# What You Should Never Do During a Divorce

There are a few things that you should never do during the divorce process.

## First, do not ask others to pick sides.

Whether it is family, friends, neighbors or co-workers, it is important for you to clarify their role in the lives of you, your spouse and your children during the divorce process. Be clear to them that you need them to support the family during this loss, to be listeners rather than expert advisers, and to not speak negatively in front of or within hearing distance of the children.

## Second, do not tell everyone you know about your spouse's affair.

While an affair causes extreme feelings of hurt and betrayal, your best course of action is to work through your emotions with an individual counselor. Discussing it publically will only make it more difficult to settle the case and will do irreparable harm to your children emotionally and mentally.

## Finally, do not discuss the divorce process with your children.

This applies regardless of their age. Find friends, other adult family members or a counselor to talk to during the process. It is important to have a sounding board and an opportunity to work through feelings, but discussing the divorce process with your children is inappropriate.

# CHAPTER 3:

# TELLING

# THE CHILDREN

# How to Tell the Children

> *If you have children, you should NEVER talk about the possibility or certainty of divorce in front of the children until the two of you, as the parents, have made the decision and can tell the children together.*

Sometimes, the adult, husband or wife in you will want to tell the children separately from your spouse about the divorce. That is the adult in you that wants to do that, not the parent. The parent in you recognizes and understands that it is going to be incredibly important for the two of you to tell the children together and to create a plan for how and when to tell the children. Just as the two of you set the tone for your divorce, the two of you also set the tone for how the children will handle the divorce.

# When to Tell the Children

> *Once the decision has been made that you are going to divorce, the two of you, as parents, need to decide when to tell the children. It will be important that your children have time to process the information rather than rushing off to school or an extracurricular event.*

You should consider waiting until the weekend (Saturday or Sunday) to tell the children. The conversation should take place earlier in the day rather than later. Ideally, both of you should be present for the conversation and both of you should participate in the conversation. This conversation is not a time for arguing, blaming, or dredging up past misgivings; it is a time for Mom and Dad to be there for their children during a difficult moment. Both of you should commit to not disparaging the other parent when telling the children. It is okay if one or both of you become tearful. If you become too overwhelmed, excuse yourself, recover and then return to the conversation.

The conversation with the children should take place prior to either parent moving out. Do not be surprised if the children are worried about the parent that is moving. They may ask questions about where that parent will be living, whether it will be close by, when they will be able to see them after they move, etc. Be prepared in advance as to how you will answer those questions together as the parents.

28

# Where to Tell the Children

Parents should tell the children at home, if at all possible, instead of in a public setting. If the child or children have been seeing a therapist, the therapist's office may offer additional support for the children. Consider discussing with the therapist whether it would be better to have the conversation in their office or at home.

# What to Tell the Children

The two of you should plan and discuss, ahead of time, what will be said to the children. In an ideal setting, the two of you would practice saying your words out loud to each other or to someone close to you so that you have at least said it once out loud. It is imperative that you both tell them that they are not responsible for the divorce and that both parents love them.

Give the children time to process the information in the way that their little hearts will process it. Sometimes children process it right then; however, often it takes children up until bedtime to ask questions, or even days later. Ideally, both parents should be present throughout the remainder of the day so that the children can come to them for support and to answer questions.

Children will likely experience a variety of emotions after hearing the news, such as denial, abandonment, preoccupation with information, anger/hostility, depression, preoccupation with reconciliation, blame, guilt, acting out, and stages of grief. Younger children (ages three to five) may ask if they caused the divorce. They will have questions such as where are they going to live, who are they going to live with, and who will take them to games and other events. You should be prepared to answer general questions with age appropriate responses. If you do not know the answer to a question that they have asked, let them know that you don't know the answer yet but that as you know you will let them know. If changes are coming, prepare them in an age appropriate manner.

During this time, be careful that you do not tell the children that something is going to be a certain way when you do not really know that yet. Early in the divorce process, you do not know if one spouse will continue to live in the house or if it will be sold. You do not know how the parenting time schedule will work out. There may be things that you "hope" will happen (I want to continue to live in the house), but make sure you only convey facts to the children (Mommy and Daddy will be deciding where we will each live. We do not know yet.). Also, NEVER discuss adult matters with the children. This includes the financial settlement, affairs or sexual issues, or custody arrangements.

29

*In the days following the news, the children may approach you*

*with questions. Again, reassure them that it is not their fault.*

*It is important to support them through any necessary changes,*

*but try to make as few changes as possible and stick to their routines.*

*Make sure they see both of you as often as possible.*

## What NOT to Tell the Children
### Here is a list of tips for what not to tell the children,
courtesy of Between Two Homes®, LLC (www.childreninthemiddle.com).

It is important for parents to know and understand the power that their words have with children. It will be incredibly important going forward that words spoken allow the children to love both parents. I always tell parents, "If what is about to come out of your mouth will make your children have to decide between right parent/wrong parent, good parent/bad parent, do not say it. Rethink it and say it in a way that allows your children to love both of you.

**Do not say:** "I do not love him or her anymore so it is best we do this." On a very basic level children see themselves as half Mom and half Dad. I have actually experienced a child saying, 'Mom said she doesn't love Dad anymore. Is there a chance she will stop loving me?'

**Do not say:** "Mommy and Daddy still love you and it will be just like it's always been except we live in different homes." Things will not be just like they have always been. They will not be able to see each of you every day. They will not have the same experience of having both parents in one home ever again.

**Do not say:** "Remember how we disagreed on how we should take care of you, well now we are going to let the judge decide who was right." Remember, children should never have to decide who is right and who is wrong, or who is good and who is bad. The ultimate decision of how your children are parented is up to the two of you, unless you show the court the two of you cannot create a parenting plan that is in the best interest of the children. If you cannot, then the judge will make a decision and it will not support either of you being right or being wrong. It will be the judge's plan for your family, not yours.

**Do not say:** "Everything will be all right, you'll see." In their little hearts and minds things will not seem all right for many years to come. Based on the level of conflict you and your spouse go through, it could take your children years if not a lifetime to recover. On the same note, staying together in a high conflict marriage can also create a lifetime of recovery for your children. Studies have shown that children fair better when their high conflict parents divorce rather than their parents staying together. Things will not be all right.

**Do not say:** "You can still see them whenever you want." If the two of you are living next door to each other with a swinging gate in between your homes this may be true. Or if you live across the street from each other, this may be true. Otherwise chances are there will be days that your children see each of you but rarely both of you. Unfortunately this may be a reality of their lives going forward.

**Do not say:** "I will have my time with you, and he/she will have their time with you." Unfortunately professionals who work with families going through a divorce have seen that when these statements are made, it means that the children have to adjust to the parents' schedules rather than the parents continuing to adjust to the children's schedules as they did when everyone lived under one roof. The children will still have the same schedule and it is still not "your time". Your life will continue to revolve around your children's schedules. It is a large concern to specialists when we see parents saying no to birthday parties, extracurricular activities and othe events because it is "their time".

Reprinted with permission from Between Two Homes®, LLC, (www.childreninthemiddle.com).

# CHAPTER 4:

# STAGES OF DIVORCE:

# EMOTIONAL, FINANCIAL,

# LEGAL & SOCIAL

# EMOTIONAL STAGES

*Outside of the death of a loved one, experts consider divorce to be one of the toughest, life changing experiences a person could go through. Researchers have determined that divorce is so impactful that the widely accepted five stages of grief can be applied to the divorce experience.*

"The Five Stages of Grief" developed by David Kessler and Elisabeth Kubler-Ross are defined as: **Denial/Shock, Anger, Depression, Bargaining and Acceptance.**
Those five stages can be applied to each stage of the divorce process.

## Denial/Shock

Shock that the marriage is over, denial that there has been an affair, denial that the love no longer exists. There is an illusion that everything is ok, we will get through this, it is not happening to us, we are not one of those couples, we will work things out.

## Anger

Anger over the affair, anger at the other spouse for disconnecting, anger about how this will hurt the children, anger over the loss of the dream. The anger includes being angry at oneself and angry at the other spouse. Blaming often happens.

## Depression

A mild to intense sadness over the loss of the love, the loss of the dream, sadness for the children, mourning, the erosion is felt so deeply.

## Bargaining

If only I could have been a better partner, kept the house cleaner, made more money, been more attractive, cooked more, not gained weight, parented the children better. I will make a nice dinner and we can reconnect, I will start working out, I will hire a maid, I will work more hours to bring in more money.

## Acceptance

This is happening to us, this is happening to me, this is happening to our children and we will get through it. I am going to be single. I am going to be a single parent. I am no longer stressed all of the time. I look forward to figuring out who I am absent the other person.

A very common situation seen by those who work with families going through divorce is where one spouse has spent months or years working their way through the emotional stages of divorce, while still in the marriage and without the other spouse knowing. These people have already made it to the acceptance stage. Then they file for divorce and ONLY THEN can the other spouse begin working through the emotional stages of divorce.

For the person who has just been caught off guard, surprised by the news of divorce, it is extremely difficult. They are beginning the stages of grief, and in the midst of grief, they begin trying to work their way through the family law court system. The last place someone would want to be, in the middle of grieving such a tremendous loss, is in a courtroom, litigating (fighting out) their divorce.

What we know for sure is that even good people, when hurting enough, alter their behavior in an effort to survive traumatic experiences. We will be talking about alternatives to the litigated divorce later in this book.

# FINANCIAL STAGES

It is usually very hard to separate the financial decisions that need to be made from the intense emotions felt during the divorce process. However, it is very important to try to make rational, educated financial decisions instead of irrational, emotional decisions during the process.

It may be helpful to find a neutral third party who understands finances to help advise you on financial decisions during the divorce. This person should NOT be a family member or friend who hates your spouse. This needs to be a person who has no ties to the situation and who can remain calm and level-headed during the process.

## The financial stages of the process include:

1.  Identify all the assets and liabilities.

2.  With your attorney, start to identify what may be separate property and what may be marital (or community) property.

3.  Create a detailed list of estimated post divorce income and expenses. Some items may be known and some may be unknown.

4.  Evaluate various options for splitting the assets and liabilities, as well as various options for post divorce income and expenses.

5.  Work through difficult issues such as what to do with your home and the family business.

6.  Narrow down the options to what is reasonable and realistic.

7.  Achieve a financial settlement that is acceptable to both spouses.

# LEGAL STAGES
### There are three legal stages of divorce.

## Phase One

Deciding to divorce and filing. In order to legally begin the divorce process you must file a "Petition for Divorce". This is the document that informs the Court and your spouse legally that you are seeking a divorce. It will not typically include any gory details or reasons why you want a divorce. It will not typically include a detailed listing of how you want to divide the assets. It may generally state who you think the children should live with most of the time, but it usually would not state details as to why. There is a sixty day waiting period in Texas after the filing of the petition for divorce before you can finalize your divorce (other states may be different). Typically it takes longer than sixty days to resolve a case, but it could be resolved that quickly in some instances.

## Phase Two

The "temporary" phase. This is the phase between filing for divorce and finalizing the divorce. At the beginning of this phase, a temporary parenting time schedule will need to be determined. This can be done by agreement or by the Court if the parents cannot reach their own agreement. This will not be the permanent plan post-divorce. This is only the temporary plan while the divorce is pending. Additionally, decisions need to be made about how bills will be paid and who will live in the house during this phase. These decisions can also be made by agreement or by the Court.

## Phase Three

This is the "permanent" phase. Once the temporary orders are in place, you will begin working on the final decisions. This will include the permanent parenting time schedule for the children and how the assets and debts will be divided. In addition, you will be working on whether child support or spousal support (alimony) will be paid post-divorce and, if so, by whom and how much.

In order to help you work these things out, you may select a settlement process such as collaborative or mediation (there is further discussion of divorce process options later in the book). If you do not reach an agreement with your spouse, there will be a trial and the Judge will make those decisions for you. Most cases settle because taking your case to trial is very expensive and most people would prefer to decide their own fate rather than putting it in a Judge's hands.

**37**

# SOCIAL STAGES

## Picking Sides

We find it disappointing and amazing how many friends of those divorcing feel like they have to pick sides during a divorce. Most of the time this behavior is unsolicited. Also, some church denominations hold the spiritual belief that "divorce is not an option" so people going through a divorce may be disenfranchised from the congregation. It is an unfortunate side effect that in the midst of one of the most significant losses during a person's lifetime, people also must experience the loss of their friends, neighbors, in-laws and even church home.

Both spouses need as much support as possible during this time and beyond. It is important for them to tell friends, neighbors, in-laws, and their church that both of them need their support.

As you go through the divorce process, be aware that you may be forced to say goodbye to the support system that you have had and begin seeking out a new support system.

## The New "Single Me"

In the midst of a difficult marital relationship, sometimes the fear of what life will be like post-divorce can seem worse than staying in an unhealthy relationship. Fear of the unknown is one reason people tend to stay in marriages too long. From a social aspect, you may be losing the person who has been your best friend, your roommate, and your social companion. You may now be coming home to an empty house, spending more time alone, and going to more places by yourself. It is normal to feel lonely.

As you work through the transition to being single again, it is important to slow down, to allow yourself time to think and heal, and to take care of yourself. Use this experience as an opportunity to reconnect with yourself and become your own best friend. You may feel like you lost your identity during the marriage or are losing your identity during the divorce process.

## Ask yourself the following questions:

- Who am I?

- What are my greatest strengths?

- What do I want to do with my life?

- What activities make me happy?

- What do I like to do for fun?

- Are there things I always wanted to do, but my spouse would never agree to do them with me?

- Are there classes I would like to take to learn new things?

- Are there groups related to hobbies or sports or common interests that I would like to join?

- Do I want to get more involved in charitable activities or religious organizations?

**This is a time to create a new, full, and rewarding life for yourself.**

Identify friends and family members who are positive and supportive, but also be open to making new friends. Join a support group of others who are going through a similar situation. The most important thing to remember is not to isolate yourself.

Be open to new activities and new people, but don't rush into any new commitments. Although people have a natural tendency to want to begin a new relationship immediately and eliminate the uncomfortable feelings of loneliness, force yourself to stay single and uncommitted for a period of time.

# The New Single Parent

The life of parenting as you know it is going to change. You will not only be managing the new single you, but you will be managing the new jobs of single parenting and co-parenting. There will be more responsibilities, scheduling challenges, a new household to set up and maintain, and conversations with the children about their grief and healing.

Time with your children will need to be focused on them. The first year will be challenging. Just know that the first year is not indicative of how the future will be. You will eventually settle into a schedule and rhythm that works for all of you. Find other single parents who have made it through the first year and ask them to share their experiences with you.

> *Remember, finding a positive support network will help life transition in a smoother manner.*

# For The Children

Social life for the children is going to change as well. Identifying themselves as children of divorce may be difficult. Ideally, you and your children's other parent will choose to live close enough to each other so that the children's lives can maintain as much normalcy as possible. It is our hope that you will support your children by allowing them to participate in the same activities that they have in the past.

Should the two of you, as parents, choose not to live close to each other, the children's lives will be impacted more substantially. The further the distance between their two homes, the more challenges your children will face. Distance will add the challenges of having a different set of friends at Mom's house and at Dad's house. It may also impact the children's ability to participate in their regular activities, or in any activities, if the driving distance is unreasonable.

> *It is our belief that if you choose to relocate to an area that is not close to the children's other home, you should remain committed to helping the children stay connected to all of their friends and to continue to participate in all of the activities they are involved in.*

# CHAPTER 5:

# MENTAL HEALTH
# READINESS

# The Benefits of Counseling

*Everyone can benefit from counseling during the divorce process.*

People going through a divorce are generally good people going through one of the worst times in their lives. The process of divorce itself creates intense emotions. Things that normally would not bother you will turn your day upside down. Unfortunately, some people develop destructive behaviors as ways of coping. Destructive behaviors might include alcohol, drugs, promiscuity, gambling, spending sprees, and revenge/vengeance.

It is normal to need additional support during the course of a divorce. There is no shame in asking for support from a counselor. Counseling sessions provide a confidential and safe place to talk, where you can work through emotions, brainstorm better ways to handle situations, and role play difficult conversations. It can provide a different type of support than what you might get from a friend, family member, neighbor or co-worker.

Be open to the idea that anti-depressant or anti-anxiety medications may be needed during the divorce process. It would not be uncommon to need this additional medical support. Remember, outside of the loss of a loved one, divorce is one of the most difficult things to go through in life. When talk therapy is not enough, anti-depressant or anti-anxiety medications may be necessary for you to be able focus on the divorce process, major life decisions, the children and your job. Please consult with your physician or therapist if you are considering or have questions about taking anti-depressants or anti-anxiety medications.

## How to Find a Good Counselor

*It is important that you find a reputable counselor to work with during your divorce. The best resources we've found include the Texas Counseling Association, American Counseling Association, local colleges and universities, your family law attorney, or others who work with divorcing families.*

# Children, Grief and Counseling

Children will also experience a lot of emotions and the five stages of grief during this transition. Just as it takes adults time to navigate through the emotions associated with divorce, it will take the children time as well.

*We suggest that all parents going through divorce strongly consider taking their children to counseling so that they have a safe, neutral, third party with whom they can process through their emotions.*

We are hoping that you will provide your children the tools and support they need to be able to process through their grief in a healthy manner. A counselor is someone they can trust who is not Mom or Dad. Counseling will allow them to share all of their feelings in a safe environment without feeling like they have to say what Mom or Dad wants them to hear.

After several months, if your children appear to still be struggling with the changes that have taken place, you should definitely seek professional counseling for them. You may notice that they still seem emotionally impacted or are showing any of the following signs: withdrawal, anger, regressive behaviors (a seven year old starts sucking their thumb again or a nine year old starts wetting the bed), problems sleeping, problems at school, self-injury, over eating/under eating, or a decline in enjoying activities they once enjoyed.

The children may tell you that they do not want to go. Insist that they go at least once and let them know that they can go as many times as they would like to. Listen to the counselor's feedback about the continuing need for sessions and the appropriate frequency.

If the divorce or events surrounding the divorce have caused the children to be especially resentful toward one parent, estranged, or have severely damaged the parent-child relationship, we recommend pursuing counseling sessions to begin to rebuild the relationship. Parenting itself is not easy and divorce adds an extra layer to the challenges of parenting.

# Children & Co-Parenting

The best possible outcome for the children is no exposure to divorce conflict. It is a critical commitment that parents must keep in order for the children to continue to feel important and loved. When children are exposed to the conflict, they may experience feelings of guilt (they did something wrong), feeling like they have to pick sides, and feeling like they are stuck in the middle, unimportant and alone.

The following items in the appendix are fantastic ones for reviewing and/or renewing your commitment to protecting your children from the harmful effects of divorce.

- Children's Bill of Rights – *Appendix 1*
- Rules For Co-Parenting – *Appendix 2*

# Co-Parenting Classes

*Many courts now require that divorcing parents participate in co-parenting classes prior to finalizing the divorce. Even if you are not required by the court to take a co-parenting class, we strongly encourage you to do so.*

Co-parenting is a new skill that needs to be learned. It is not something that we naturally know how to do. Take advantage of co-parenting classes and resources to help you and your children's other parent make the divorce transition as easy as possible for your children. The classes are filled with information that will help you mentally prepare and set the stage for being the best co-parent you can be.

For a list of internet based Co-Parenting Classes, see *Appendix 3.*

For a list of internet based Co-Parenting Support Tools, see *Appendix 4.*

# Communication

It is usually better to over communicate than to under communicate. However, you and your spouse may have lost the ability to effectively communicate with each other during your marriage or during the divorce process. If you have children and will have an on-going co-parenting relationship post-divorce, it may be helpful to find a counselor to help you design a communication plan that works for both of you.

There are some other general suggestions that may help. First, do not make assumptions about what your spouse (or ex-spouse) did or did not do. Ask for clarification, repeat what you have heard, state and re-state to be sure you have been heard correctly. Likewise, think through how your spouse (or ex-spouse) might misinterpret your actions and try to over-communicate to prevent unnecessary arguments. As an example, if you take the box of baby memorabilia to your parent's house for safekeeping without discussing it with your spouse, it can fuel a sense of mistrust that affects other parts of the divorce negotiations or your relationship.

*We have also found that some divorced or soon-to-be-divorced couples do best by limiting their communication to email or text message only.*

# Parenting Time

Do not be opposed to a parenting schedule that gives each parent 50 percent of the parenting time just because you think you should receive child support. Alternatively, do not make decisions about parenting time in order to avoid paying child support. It is incredibly important to the success of your children that they have as much contact with each of you as possible (barring any domestic violence/chemical/drug abuse issues).

*Decisions about parenting time schedules should always be made based on the realities of the situation and what is in the best interest of your children.*

# CHAPTER 6:

# FINANCIAL

# READINESS

*For many people,*
*divorce is the largest financial transaction of their life.*

Depending on your knowledge of finances and the length of your marriage, the financial aspects of divorce can be overwhelming. However, it is important to look at the positive side of the situation.

*A divorce forces people to identify their assets, liabilities,*
*and cash flow and to gain a better understanding*
*of their financial situation.*

If you are thinking about divorce or have decided to divorce, there are a number of things you can begin doing to prepare for the financial aspects of the process.

# Here is a list of assets that you may have:

- Bank accounts
- Investment accounts
- Real estate, mineral interests
- Retirement accounts (including IRA, 401k, 403b, 457, pension, etc).
- Life insurance policies (individual and through employer)
- Stock options and restricted stock
- Annuities
- Business interests
- Safe deposit box contents
- Offsite storage facility contents
- Vehicles, motorcycles, boats, jet skis, RVs, airplanes
- Antiques, artwork, collections
- Memberships
- Frequent flyer miles, travel rewards and credit card points
- Pets and livestock
- Receivables from others
- 529 College Savings Plan accounts
- Custodial accounts for children (Uniform Transfer to Minors Act UTMA)
- Tax return carry forwards

# Here is a list of liabilities that you may have:

- Mortgages
- Lines of credit
- Vehicle loans
- Credit cards
- Unpaid taxes
- Unpaid bills (excluding normal monthly bills)
- Amounts owed to other people

# Credit Report

Obtain credit reports for each spouse. A credit report is an important part of the divorce process. It is used to identify all open credit card and liability accounts. It also shows whether each account is titled jointly or in one person's name. All open accounts will need to be listed in the decree and outstanding balances will need to be addressed. In addition, any mortgage, auto loan, or credit cards titled jointly require special consideration.

There are many websites available to obtain your credit report, including those of the three credit reporting agencies – Experian, Equifax and TransUnion. We recommend using the website AnnualCreditReport.com which is the only authorized source for the free annual credit report that is yours by law. The Fair Credit Reporting Act guarantees you access to your credit report at no charge from each of the three credit reporting agencies every twelve months. You do not need to purchase your credit score for divorce purposes, just obtain your free credit report.

# Financial Education

In all marriages there is a division of responsibilities. If your spouse has handled all of the financial matters, begin educating yourself about bank accounts, investments, retirement accounts, credit cards, etc. What accounts do you and your spouse have? What are the current expenses of your household and your lifestyle? What are the financial implications of your future goals?

You do not need to be embarrassed if handling the finances was not your role and therefore you are unaware of what you have or you are uncomfortable in this area. It is very common for one spouse to handle the financial matters and for the other spouse to be relatively uninformed.

# Employment

If you have not worked in recent years, begin thinking about where you would like to work post-divorce and whether additional education or training will be necessary. Unless your estate consists of millions of dollars, you will likely need to work post-divorce. It will not benefit you in the divorce process to be unemployed. It will benefit you much more in the process to have employment or to be seeking employment.

**Myth Buster:** There is a myth or misunderstanding that if you are unemployed you are more likely to be awarded alimony upon divorce. That is NOT TRUE in Texas. You are only hurting yourself by failing to seek and obtain employment.

# Health Insurance
## There are various options for health insurance post-divorce.

- You can obtain health insurance through your employer. Divorce is a qualifying event that allows you to join the employer plan mid-year, instead of having to wait until the open enrollment period.

- You can continue coverage for a limited time under your ex-spouse's employer plan under a provision known as COBRA. The maximum time to utilize COBRA following a divorce is thirty-six months and you will have to pay the related premiums, which are often higher than an individual health plan. You must notify the plan administrator of a qualifying event within sixty days after the divorce is final.

- You can apply for an individual health insurance policy. It may take four to six weeks before you are notified about whether you are approved so apply early.

- If you do not qualify for individual health insurance due to current or previous medical conditions, states generally make health insurance available through a high-risk pool. This coverage tends to be more expensive than an individual policy.

- During the divorce process you can remain on your spouse's health insurance, and your spouse will normally be legally prohibited from cancelling your health insurance until the divorce is final.

*(Note: At the time of writing this book, there is significant new healthcare legislation that may change some of this information. Please consult an appropriate resource for current information.)*

# Things Not to Do

*There are some financial actions and behaviors*
*that we recommend you avoid during the divorce process.*

## Do not spend money on a new boyfriend/girlfriend until you are divorced.

Courts and spouses frown on any monies spent on a girlfriend or boyfriend, or monies spent for you to be with your girlfriend or boyfriend. For example, perhaps you did not buy her dinner but you bought your own dinner while you were with her - that is still a problem. And the problem is not proportional to the amount spent. In other words, some divorcing people have said, "It was not that much money, maybe altogether it was $900 and we have much more money than that." The amount of money spent is irrelevant.

> *Any money spent that relates*
> *to another man or woman causes problems.*

One way it causes problems is that it gives the angry betrayed spouse something to look for, be mad about, focus on, point out, talk about, point out again, ask the girlfriend about in her deposition, ask her spouse about in discovery, tell the judge about, tell the collaborative team about, tell the mediator about, tell the arbitrator about, etc. They also think there must be much more than what they found. If they found $900, in their minds that means there was really $9,000 spent, but you just did a better job hiding the rest of it.

**The ways people get caught are** bank records, credit card records, phone records including texting history and toll tag records. Statements for travel award programs and frequent flyer miles can also provide documentation of your activities. Your spouse can also ask your new girlfriend or boyfriend under oath in a deposition or at a hearing on the stand.

54

In collaborative cases there is less focus on historical behavior and more focus on the future. In collaborative cases there are no depositions or hearings and therefore no embarrassing questions of the paramour. However, even in collaborative, it is more difficult to strike a favorable deal quickly and efficiently if we have to deal with all of the emotion and fallout related to an affair and money spent on the new boyfriend/girlfriend.

> *There is a theory that some people get caught having an affair intentionally because they are too fearful to end their marriage and are instead trying to force the other person to do so (perhaps even unconsciously).*

This theory was developed after years of seeing smart people conceal their activity very poorly. Examples of this behavior might include leaving the other woman's underwear in the family laundry, using a joint credit card for obvious purchases such as Victoria's Secret or a secret post office box. If you are going to go to the trouble of getting a secret post office box, why would you pay for it each month with a joint credit card that you know your husband checks?

The issue of a new boyfriend/girlfriend is going to cost you a lot of additional money to deal with – in attorney's fees, professional fees in collaborative cases and court costs. This is going to cause your spouse to focus on something that makes you appear to be evil and makes them the victim. Therefore, if you are reading this and it is not too late, do not spend money on a new girlfriend or boyfriend or on yourself to be with them. If it is too late, stop now and at least minimize the situation as much as possible. Courts hate it and judges will penalize you for it, although the penalties are never as much as the angry betrayed spouse would like.

## Do not raid the accounts (usually).

Some people remove all of the money from the joint bank accounts prior to filing for divorce. Some people remove half of it. They do this because they are afraid the other person will remove all of the money and they are beating them to the punch, so to speak.

Only in very rare and limited circumstances is removing any money advisable. Unless it is absolutely necessary, the backlash from your spouse and the ill effects on the divorce process are not worth it. When you empty the accounts you are declaring war. You are greatly diminishing the likelihood of a civil, amicable, efficient, and less expensive divorce. You should first consider the true likelihood that your spouse will empty the accounts. Also, keep in mind that in some counties a standing order is issued upon filing for divorce which would order your spouse NOT to empty the accounts.

You do, however, need access to enough money or credit to cover your own expenses for up to a month and to pay a lawyer's retainer fee. In a worst case scenario where you do not empty the accounts but your spouse does, your lawyer will schedule a hearing, typically within a few weeks, and the judge will likely order your spouse to return the money to the joint accounts or will order your spouse to provide you with a defined amount of money each month until the case is finalized and the money is ultimately divided.

## Do not hold money in your business to keep it from your spouse.

If you have a business, part of the divorce process will be a business valuation and review of the business financial statements. Holding cash in your business in an effort to keep it from your spouse does more harm than good. It makes it appear that you are acting in bad faith and it can hurt an already cash strapped family.

## Do not take on new debt if you can avoid it.

Some people must use credit cards to pay for attorney's fees or other extra expenses that come up during the divorce process. However, it is best to minimize the amount of new debt that you incur. It is also advisable not to make any large purchases or large financial commitments until you know what the overall financial settlement will be.

## Do not insist on a settlement that is not financially feasible.

Sometimes people go into the divorce process with a certain outcome in mind. They want a certain percentage of the estate, a certain amount of support or a certain parenting time schedule. With regard to the financial settlement, there is a certain range of outcomes that is reasonable. Be willing to listen to your attorney and a neutral financial professional about whether what you want is financially feasible. If it is not feasible, do not deplete the estate further paying attorneys' fees to fight over it. This is usually a fear based or anger based position.

## Do not change your beneficiaries until after the divorce is final.

If you want to change your beneficiary designations, you need to do so either before the divorce is filed or after the divorce is finalized because in many cases the Court will issue a standing order that prohibits you from doing so. Also, in many cases you cannot change the beneficiary from your current spouse without your spouse's written consent because of community property laws in nine states, including Texas. The most common practice is to update your beneficiary designations after the divorce is finalized.

## Do not change the credit card limits, with some exceptions.

When you file for divorce, many counties will issue a standing order which will specifically prohibit you from changing the credit card limits. There are two ways a person may want to alter the credit card limits – up or down. If you want to reduce the credit card limits to restrict your spouse's ability to run up the balances, you should talk to your attorney about other ways to accomplish this goal. Usually reducing credit limits will hurt your credit score, so it is typically not in your best interest to do so. Alternatively, you may want to increase your credit card limits to potentially improve your credit score and to have more credit available to you after the divorce is complete. It is generally best to keep everything status quo until the divorce is final; however, if you have specific reasons to increase or decrease credit card limits, discuss it with your attorney, a neutral financial professional or your spouse.

# Business Valuations

What if the biggest asset in the divorce is your business? There are generally three ways to handle the business. One is that both parties continue to co-own the business.

*Since the two of you do not get along well enough anymore to remain married, it is unlikely that you can realistically co-own a business together post-divorce.*

Another option is to sell the business and split the proceeds. This is usually not a realistic option because the business is likely a significant source of the family's income and it may not be that easy to sell. The third and most likely option is that one spouse keeps the business and buys out the other spouse. This is when a business valuation is needed. For example, let's say that Fred and Wilma own Bedrock Construction Company. Fred runs the business. Wilma does not work in the business, but the business was started during their marriage and she would certainly like some value out of it.

In litigation and in collaborative cases, there are professionals that can be hired to value the business for divorce purposes. A valuation for divorce purposes is different than a valuation for any other purpose. Special rules apply. Wilma and Fred could agree (and would likely do so in a collaborative case) to hire a neutral business valuation expert. Or Wilma and Fred could each hire their own business valuator (otherwise known as competing experts).

Certain factors are considered that have a significant effect on the ultimate valuation amount. One factor is the degree to which Fred is a key player in the business, especially in service businesses such as lawyers, doctors, and CPAs. For example, let's say that Fred was really a lawyer and his firm was called Fred Flint, Attorney at Law. People came to Fred to hire him because of Fred's reputation. If Fred left the business, it would be difficult for the business to continue because the clients are loyal to Fred and would likely follow Fred to another firm. On the other hand, let's say Fred was a partner in a large law firm called Stone and Pebble which had hundreds of lawyers. People hired the firm, not because of Fred, but because of the reputation of the firm. In this example, it would be easier to value Fred's partnership interest in Stone and Pebble because he could likely sell it more easily.

Other factors that may affect the value of the business interest include what similar businesses have sold for, the discounted net cash flows of the business, the value of the assets, whether it is a controlling interest or a minority interest, and how likely it is that anyone would actually want to purchase the business interest.

# Advantages of a Financial Professional
## in Collaborative Cases

If you choose to use the collaborative model for your divorce (discussed in more depth later in the book), there are a number of benefits to including a Financial Professional as part of the collaborative team.

> *Many attorneys will not participate in a collaborative case unless it is a "full team" that includes a Mental Health Professional and a Financial Professional.*

1. The Financial Professional gathers all the financial information and documents, reviews the information, and puts it into reports that are useful to the team and the clients. Having one neutral Financial Professional to handle the financial information allows the attorneys to focus on the bigger picture, creates efficiencies and saves money on fees.

2. During option development, the Financial Professional can provide ideas and feedback in the best interest of the family without the restriction of only representing one of the parties.

3. During divorce when trust is low, spouses frequently have trouble believing what the other spouse says about their financial accounts, financial history or financial future. This is especially true when one spouse has a strong financial background and has always handled the family finances. The non-financial spouse needs to hear financial information from an independent third party in order to feel comfortable.

4. In cases where one spouse has a strong financial background and the other spouse has limited financial knowledge, it is helpful for the Financial Professional to educate the non-financial spouse on financial issues to keep the process moving in an efficient and cost effective manner.

5. Depending on the specifics of the case, offline meetings with the two clients and the Financial Professional may be used to work through issues and reach tentative agreements without holding a full team meeting or paying fees to four professionals during that time.

# How to Find a Good Financial Professional for Your Divorce

**It is important that you work with a qualified and reputable financial professional during your divorce. The person should hold one or more of the following professional credentials:**

- Certified Public Accountant (CPA)

- CERTIFIED FINANCIAL PLANNER ™ (CFP®)

- Certified Divorce Financial Analyst ™ (CDFA™ )

In addition, he or she should have experience and specific training in divorce matters.

If you are using the collaborative approach, your attorney and your spouse's attorney will usually select the neutral financial professional for your case.

If you are looking for a financial professional outside of the collaborative process, ask your attorney or other professionals for referrals in your area.

# CHAPTER 7:

## LEGAL

## READINESS

# How to Pick a Lawyer
### Here are some things we think you should look for when choosing a lawyer to represent you during the divorce process.

## Is the Lawyer's practice primarily focused on family law?
The law changes continuously. A lawyer that focuses his or her practice in one area is more likely to be up to speed on recent changes in the law, the preferences of the judges, the current practices in each court, and the alternative dispute resolution processes such as collaborative, mediation and arbitration.

## Is the lawyer well regarded by his or her peers?
Lawyers see each other's work product every day when we have cases together. We see each other's written work product and performance in the courtroom and in collaborative meetings. Lawyers know better than anyone who is ethical and who is not. They know who is smart and hardworking, and who is not. One way to find this out is to call a few divorce lawyers and ask them who the top three lawyers are that they would hire besides themselves and their firm.

## Has the lawyer been in trouble with the state bar association?
In Texas, you would go to www.texasbar.com and enter the lawyer's name to see if he or she has been the recipient of any public sanctions or disciplinary action.

## Spend the time and money to interview two to three lawyers.

Family law is very personal and you should feel comfortable with the lawyer you decide to hire. Observe how responsive the lawyer and their staff are during this initial contact. The number one complaint against lawyers is the failure to call their clients back in a timely manner. How the lawyer handles your initial contact could give you an indication of whether or not that lawyer and their firm are prompt in their attentiveness to client needs.

## Ask the lawyers you interview various questions, such as:

What percentage of your practice is family law? What is likely to be their approach to your case based on the facts you have given them? Do they practice in both collaborative and litigation models? Do they feel more comfortable in collaborative or litigated cases?

**BE AWARE** that some lawyers are advising potential clients away from the collaborative approach, only because the lawyer is not comfortable with their own skill set in the collaborative approach or is not trained in it. However, they do not want to lose the business and therefore they advise the client that litigation is the best path for them, even if it is not.

## How long has the lawyer been practicing?

If it is under five years, do they have a mentor?

# How to Keep Legal Fees Reasonable

**Divorce is expensive.** There is a certain amount of work that has to be done by the lawyers, financial professionals, and mental health professionals with whom you are working in order to fulfill their professional duties. Some lawyers have a reputation for churning the file to generate extra fees, but most try to resolve your case in an efficient, but thorough manner. There are, however, ways that you can help to minimize the amount of fees.

In every case, there is a phase of information gathering. In litigation cases this is called discovery and in collaborative cases it is one of the early steps on the Roadmap to Resolution.

> *One important cost saving measure is to provide all of the information that is requested and to provide it in an orderly manner.*

Financial information is one of the main categories of information gathering. This includes bank statements, credit card statements, deeds and closing documents for real estate, and so on. You will save fees by providing this information in a timely, chronological and orderly state. As an example, create a folder for each bank account and put the statements in date order from oldest to newest. If you are missing any statements, indicate that with a sticky note. Also, make copies of your original documents for the professionals. Do not incur the cost of their firms making copies of your documents and returning the originals to you. We all know that gathering the financial documents is a pain. However, be mindful of what you can do to make it as quick and easy as possible for the professionals to work through your documents.

*A second way to keep costs down is to be on your best behavior and try your best to treat your spouse with respect during the process.*

As we have discussed in other chapters, behaviors such as withdrawing all the money from the bank accounts, having a boyfriend or girlfriend on the side, telling the children what a horrible person their father or mother is, or not abiding by temporary agreements can throw your case into a tailspin and cause the fees to go through the roof.

*Another way to keep costs down is to not use your lawyer as a substitute for a therapist or a friend.*

You are likely paying your lawyer a high hourly rate. The lawyer will charge you for any time spent on the phone or in person, as well as for writing, reading and replying to emails. Divorce is a major life change and you will need someone to talk to about the emotional aspect of divorcing. Try to identify a friend or hire a therapist to talk to about these things. Your lawyer is definitely willing to discuss the emotional side with you, but it is an expensive way to do it. In addition, your lawyer is trained in the law, not in psychology. A therapist will generally be a better choice for this need.

**WARNING:**
**If you decide to use a friend as your sounding board during the divorce, choose only one friend and ask that friend to keep the information completely confidential. It will not be good for your family or your case to have the details of your divorce spread throughout the neighborhood or your social circle.**

# CHAPTER 8:

# HOW TO PICK

# A DIVORCE PROCESS

There are many ways to get divorced.
Below is a description of various approaches
to help you determine the best approach
for you and your family.

## Kitchen Table Approach

In this approach one or both of you would have a lawyer. However the lawyer(s) would mainly act as a scribe. You and your spouse would sit down at the kitchen table (so to speak) and work out your deal. In other words, the two of you would tell the lawyers how you are going to divide your assets and debts, what the support payments will be (if any), how you will handle your taxes and the details of your parenting plan. In this model the lawyers usually do not do any negotiating for you. Their role is to turn your agreement into legally binding documents. These documents will include a decree of divorce, and possibly other documents such as an agreement incident to divorce, real estate documents to transfer the house, and documents to transfer the cars and/or a portion of the 401K.

**Pros: This is the least expensive process involving lawyers if you are considering attorney's fees only.**

It can be done fairly quickly if you and your spouse generally agree on things.

**Cons: This could be the most expensive process if you strike a poor financial deal for yourself or create an incomplete parenting plan or one that lacks important details for now or the future.**

Most people cannot do this effectively due to emotion and the dynamics of their relationship with their spouse. This is a poor choice if one party tends to bully the other.

# Representing Yourself (Pro Se)

In Texas and other states, you are allowed to represent yourself without using an attorney (check your state's divorce laws). You are called a "Pro Se" when you represent yourself. In order to do this, you must familiarize yourself with your state's divorce laws, as well as fill out and file all of the applicable forms yourself.

**Pros: You do not have to pay a lawyer.**

**Cons: You are held to the same rules and standards as lawyers.**

There is a reason that lawyers went to law school. The procedures and rules are not easy to sort out and it is unlikely that you will successfully sort them out. If you have a contested hearing or trial, you will be held to the rules of evidence, just like a lawyer, and it may be difficult to place the evidence before the court that you would like the judge to consider. You are likely to end up with an un-favorable result.

# Litigation Approach

This is the Court model. If you choose to pursue this model, the goal will be to settle if possible. If a settlement cannot be reached between the parties and their lawyers, the Judge will make decisions for you after a hearing or trial.

**Pros: Sometimes you and your spouse cannot reach settlement and you need a third party (a Judge) to bring resolution to your case.**

**Cons: Litigation is typically the most expensive model.**

This model is not private and usually involves more mud-slinging. Also, you do not have the neutral mental health professional and financial planner that the collaborative model provides.

# Collaborative Approach

Collaborative Law is a more civilized and respectful, interest-based approach to resolving the case outside of the court system. It typically involves two collaborative lawyers, a neutral mental health professional and a neutral financial planner.

**Pros: This is an excellent way to resolve difficult issues surrounding division of assets or custody of the children in a private, less adversarial manner.**

You and your spouse have control over the process and the outcome. The process allows the divorcing couple to come up with creative solutions for their divorce settlement and going through the process can help to increase financial knowledge and begin laying the groundwork for an effective co-parenting relationship.

**Cons: The cost is usually less expensive than the litigation model, but it is more expensive than the other non-litigated methods described above.**

This option is only available if both parties agree.

The role of a Mental Health Professional (MHP) in the Collaborative approach to divorce is to assist in communication by helping those involved in the case express themselves and listen effectively. The MHP also assists in protecting the collaborative process by encouraging all parties involved to abide by expectations of behavior that are crucial to finalizing the divorce. Finally, the MHP also helps the divorcing parents create a workable parenting plan for them and their children's future. Throughout the case, the MHP models healthy and effective communication, healthy co-parenting and conflict resolution.

To find a Mental Health Professional trained in working with individuals during divorce please see **Appendix 8**.

## Myth Buster:

Do you and your spouse have to get along well to use the Collaborative Law method? NO. The Collaborative Law method can be used in most (but not all) situations. The professionals who practice this method have been through specific training and are able to handle difficult parenting and personality issues, complex financial matters, addictions, and other challenging situations. And it allows these challenges to be handled in a private setting.

## Myth Buster:

Can a lawyer represent both the husband and wife in a divorce if everything is agreed or friendly? NO. It is ethically not allowed because it is a potential conflict of interest. The lawyer cannot represent two people against each other that have the potential to have conflicting interests. In a divorce setting, even if you think that you agree upon everything, you certainly have the potential to be in conflict. For example, you want the green couch and so does he, or you want the children on Christmas Day every year and so does she.

# CHAPTER 9:

# LIVING ARRANGEMENTS

# & THE HOUSE

# Living Arrangements During the Divorce Process

Sometimes spouses decide to continue to live in the same house during the divorce process, usually in an effort to save money. However, living together during the divorce process is very difficult. Sometimes it is important to step back and look at the big picture. As living together becomes more difficult and communication breakdowns occur, it may end up costing more in legal fees and have a negative impact on the ultimate settlement. In addition, continued fighting and miscommunication can negatively affect the children's experience and is emotionally draining.

If you do decide to live together during the process, it is important to establish ground rules. Meeting with a mental health professional may be an efficient way to establish ground rules and boundaries. Also, it is best not to discuss the case at home.

# Think Twice About Keeping the House

*One of the biggest mistakes we see is when one spouse, usually the wife, insists that he or she must keep the house.*

The most common reason that a spouse may want to keep the house is for the stability of the children. Other reasons may include that it is a tangible asset which is easy to understand, not wanting to give others the impression that you were kicked out of the house, and the misconception that a house is a good investment because prices always go up.

The person wanting to keep the house often does not realize how expensive it is to maintain. A house can be a cash flow drain. Recurring expenses include the mortgage, electric, gas, water, trash, phone, internet, cable, pest service, alarm monitoring, and lawn treatment. The big recurring items are property taxes and insurance.

Some people also hire professionals to clean the house, mow the yard, maintain the landscape, and clean the pool. And then there is the big stuff that comes up. The house needs a new roof, new air conditioner, exterior painting, a plumber, tree trimming, fence repair, etc. The regular monthly expenses are one thing, but the big unexpected items can be financially crippling.

*Remember that the family income that has been supporting one household will now be supporting two households. Each spouse needs a comfortable, but reasonably priced place to live.*

*If you still really want to keep the house, start doing your homework.*

Make a very detailed list of all the recurring monthly and quarterly expenses. Find out the average cost of each item over the last 12 months. Think about the tasks that your spouse does which you may now need to hire someone to do (i.e. lawn mowing, house cleaning, etc.). Then make a list of the occasional big expensive things that come up when you own a home. If needed, talk to parents, neighbors, or others to get their input on big ticket items that you may be forgetting.

Once you have gathered all of this information, calculate the average monthly cost of maintaining the home. Factor that number into your overall thought process about what makes sense for the divorce settlement.

If the cost of maintaining the current home is daunting, brainstorm other options to accomplish the same goal. If you want your children to attend the same school, consider other less expensive homes in the area that may be for sale. Consider renting a house in the area. Renting relieves some of the cost burden because you are not responsible for the big repairs and maintenance. It also gives you the freedom to move when your lease is up. It is much easier to pay the penalty to break a lease than it is to try to sell your house.

If the reason you want to keep the house is because it is paid off and you want the security of knowing you have somewhere to live for the rest of your life, consider whether this house is the right answer for you or if it makes more sense to downsize to a house that is more affordable for the long term. If you want to keep the house to hold on to the memories or because you do not want to let go of the idea of your family being intact, talk through these thoughts with your counselor and brainstorm other ways to keep those memories.

# CHAPTER 10:

# STRATEGIES

# FOR MOVING OUT

*A difficult experience that many divorcing couples face at some point is when one spouse moves out of the house and the other spouse remains. If children are involved, it is very important that both spouses work together and get professional advice on how to best handle this situation.*

## The first step is telling the children that Mommy or Daddy is moving out.

Depending on the situation, moving out may happen before, during or at the end of the divorce process. Therefore, moving out may not coincide with discussing divorce with the children.

Telling the children should follow parameters similar to those suggested for how to tell the children about the divorce. Both parents should be present and should present a united front. Most importantly, the children should never be told that one spouse is forcing the other to move out or that it is one spouse's fault that the other spouse has to move out.

# Children should hear from both Mom and Dad that "We've decided together that it is best for our family if Mom/Dad moves into a separate house."

When the actual packing and moving takes place, the children should not be present. They can go spend a day or a weekend with grandparents or other family. They should not have to pack boxes or move things. The parent who moves out should get things unpacked in the new place when the children are not present.

The parent in the new house can bring some excitement to the process by letting the children pick their rooms and pick out paint colors and some new decorations. Children may also give input on a few things like where the couch looks best. However, they should not have to deal with the burden of unpacking and organizing a whole house.

Planning the children's first visit to the parent's new house is important. As an example, let's say Dad has moved into a new home and Mom will continue to live in the family home. For the children's first visit, one strategy that works well is for Mom and the children to plan a Saturday lunchtime visit to Dad's new home. Mom and the children could pick up pizza or sandwiches and take them to Dad's new house. The whole family spends an hour or two at Dad's house and then Mom and the children go back to Mom's house.

Over time, the children gradually have longer and more frequent visits to Dad's house. This allows the children to ease into their new environment. It is important that Mom comes the first time. This allows the children to feel comfortable that Mom knows where they are when they are at Dad's house and it is okay. Another example would be that both parents take the children to look for new housing for the parent moving out.

# CHAPTER 11:

# CHILDREN'S EXPENSES &

# THE FINANCIAL SETTLEMENT

# Children's Expenses

## Most parents have never sat down and created a summary of how much they spend on their children. This can be a very helpful exercise, especially when facing divorce.

If you choose a litigated divorce, the child support amount ordered by the Judge will be based on your state's laws. This calculation may also be used in some other divorce processes. However, this amount may or may not be appropriate for your family situation.

As part of a collaborative divorce, the team can come up with creative options for handling expenses related to the children and can set a child support amount that is different from state law. Examples of some options:

- One parent pays child support to the other parent which is meant to cover everything.

- Neither parent pays child support, but certain specified expenses are shared.

- One parent pays all of certain specified expenses directly to the providers (i.e. daycare, private school tuition, after-school care, summer camp, sports fees, etc.).

- Each parent pays half or a portion (not necessarily half and half) of certain children's expenses directly to the providers.

- One or both parents pay certain expenses and submit receipts to the other parent for reimbursement, either full reimbursement or some percentage.

- Parents can contribute set monthly amounts to a joint bank account that is used to pay for the children's expenses.

The important thing to consider is what will be the easiest and most comfortable way to handle these expenses with your ex-spouse going forward. Some parents like to be exact, some parents are fine with "close enough". Some parents can responsibly and maturely handle a joint bank account, others cannot. Some parents would prefer to pay for things directly instead of "giving money to my ex". Some parents know they will do best if they keep future communication with each other to a minimum. Think about what will work best for you and your children's other parent.

84

# Children's Health Insurance & Expenses

Sometimes one parent is obligated to provide health insurance for the children at their own expense. Another option is that one parent is obligated to provide health insurance, but the other parent has to reimburse them for half or a percentage of the premiums.

Some parents agree to compare the health insurance cost and coverage offered by each parent's employer every year and choose the "best rate conservator" to put the children on that plan. This can be especially helpful when one or both parents will be changing jobs in the near future. The decision of whose plan the children are on is separate from who pays the premiums. The other parent can reimburse all or a percentage of the cost of premiums.

Any co-pays and out-of-pocket medical expenses can be split between the parents in half or in some percentage, or paid in full by one parent.

# College

In the collaborative process (or other settlement process), parents can choose whether or not to address paying for college in the decree of divorce. Some of the factors that may affect this decision are:

- What were you and your spouse planning to do with regard to children's college expenses while you were married?

- In a perfect world, would you like to pay for your children's college expenses in full, partially, or not at all? People have different philosophies about this.

- What is your current financial situation (i.e. can you set aside a lump sum now to cover it)?

- What is the expected future financial situation of each parent?

- Have you each saved enough for your own retirement? Financial professionals generally advise that you fund your own retirement before funding college.

- Do you trust that you and your spouse are both committed enough to the children's college education that you will be able to work it out later and do not need to address it now?

## If college is addressed in the decree of divorce, there are several ways to do it:

- One or both parents can be obligated to contribute a certain amount each month to 529 plan college savings accounts for the children (or quarterly or annually). The advantage to this method is that the amount of the obligation is known and certain.

- One parent can be 100 percent obligated to pay for college.

- Both parents can be obligated to pay for college, with some agreed upon percentage split of costs.

# Some additional things to consider if you choose to address college in the decree of divorce:

- College costs need to be clearly defined. Besides tuition and required fees, you may decide to include or exclude dorm room & board, apartment rent, books, supplies, laptop, travel, sports pass, extra spending money, etc.

- Decide whether you are paying for four years of undergraduate expenses, five years, whatever it takes for them to graduate, and/or advanced degrees.

- Will you pay for any school, only public schools, only in-state schools, etc?

- Do you want to commit to pay for these expenses in full or partially, with your child being partially responsible?

- What if your child takes one or more years "off" after high school?

It is common to include some limitations if one or both of the parents are going to obligate themselves in the decree of divorce to pay for college. For example, that they will pay for college up to the cost of the University of Texas at Austin at that time as long as the child maintains at least a C grade point average, takes at least 12 hours a semester, and the obligation expires after four years. You and your spouse can have similar limitations, create your own or choose to have none. One reason for the limitations is to guard against a scenario where your 19 year old is not attending class and she is instead smoking pot in her boyfriend's apartment, yet you are obligated to keep paying for college. You can avoid that scenario by having certain limitations.

If you are in a litigated process, under the current law the Court does not have the power to address how college will be paid for or to consider it in anyway. There is a bit of a legal fiction that once children are eighteen and have graduated from high school they are self-sufficient.

# Financial Summary

*As you work through the financial aspects of divorce,*
*make sure you think about how financial decisions*
*will affect the rest of your life.*

*Do not fall into the trap of only focusing on the period of time while*
*the children are living in your home.*

*Do not over commit to financial obligations that you cannot fulfill.*

*Some day the children will grow up and move out.*
*One of your goals should be to continue to be financially*
*self-sufficient after they are gone.*

# CHAPTER 12:

# COMMUNITY PROPERTY,

# SEPARATE PROPERTY

# & PRE-NUPS

# Definitions

## Separate Property:  A spouse's separate property consists of:

1. the property owned or claimed by the spouse before marriage;

2. the property acquired by the spouse during marriage by gift, devise, or descent; and

3. the recovery for personal injuries sustained by the spouse during marriage, except any recovery for loss of earning capacity during marriage.

## Community Property:  Community property consists of the property, other than separate property, acquired by either spouse during marriage.

## What is Community Property?

There are two types of property in a divorce case.

> *Community property is the pool of money and assets and debts that is going to be divided between you and your spouse. Separate property is not in the pool of money to be divided, but will be given to one spouse only and not counted in the division.*

It might be helpful to understand the big picture and then delve into the details of the law. Community property is that which we (you, me or us) earned while we were married. Separate property is that which had nothing to do with our marriage.

As an example, if Fred worked for the Zoo for ten years before he married Betty, the money he put into his profit sharing plan while employed at the Zoo is his separate property because Fred and Betty were not married yet and were not working together towards this financial goal.

On the other hand, let's say Fred and Betty were already married when Fred got his job at the Zoo. Fred worked for the Zoo for ten years and then Betty and Fred decided to divorce. Fred's profit sharing plan at the Zoo is community property and will be in the pool of assets to be divided. It is community property even though it is only in Fred's name and even though it is only from Fred's hard work.

The theory is that regardless of whether Fred or Betty worked for the Zoo, they were in this together. And perhaps Betty was doing things to help and support Fred that allowed him to be successful at his Zoo job. Even if Betty was hateful and not supportive and it is a miracle that Fred kept his Zoo job all these years because Betty was making his life so miserable, the profit sharing plan is still in the community property pool to be divided.

## What is Separate Property?

As you see from our formal legal definitions above, one type of separate property (if you can prove it, which we will come back to) is something that you owned prior to marriage that STILL EXISTS or can be traced into something that STILL EXISTS. If you spent it or cannot trace it, in most cases, it is gone and is not to be discussed.

As an example, let's say that Mary owned Disney stock prior to getting married and she still owns it. The Judge says that it is separate property because she owned it prior to marriage and she has documentation to prove it. The Judge has decided to divide the parties' community assets 50/50. The community pool is worth $100,000. Joe is given $50,000 and Mary is given $50,000 plus her Disney stock.

Another common type of separate property is a gift or inheritance. For example, Janie and Sam get married. Five years later, Janie's dad dies and leaves her $20,000. Janie puts that $20,000 in an account by itself and does not spend it. If they get divorced and Janie can prove with documents that this money was her inheritance, the $20,000 will be awarded to her as separate property.

What if instead Janie and Sam used the $20,000 to take an amazing trip to Africa and all the money was spent on the African Safari. The money is gone. Janie will not be able to make a claim for $20,000 of separate property. The money was spent and the Court is not going to make Sam pay her back.

# Proving Separate Property

*All property at the date of divorce is assumed to be community property unless you can prove that it is separate property. The burden to prove this is on the person who is claiming it as separate property. It can be difficult to prove if a long period of time has passed and you have not kept all of your records.*

For example, let's say that Jack and Jill were married twenty years ago. Prior to their marriage Jill worked at TXCO in the corporate office for seven years. Jill is a saver and she maxed out her 401(k) contribution during those seven years. At the date of marriage, she had about $80,000 in her 401(k). She left TXCO the day before she got married. She never touched the account and now it has grown to $600,000. Is that her separate property or is it community property or both? If she has every 401(k) statement from the month before marriage through the date of divorce then she can hire a financial forensic expert to go through them and tell the Court what portion is separate property and what portion is community property. If she does not have all of those documents then likely she cannot meet her burden and it will all be assumed to be community property. If she does have all the documents, it will likely be a mix of both, because income and dividends from separate property in most cases is community property.

## Do You Have a Pre-nup? Are They Enforceable?

Pre-nuptial agreements are enforceable. They are very difficult to challenge or set aside. The reason for this is that the courts and legislature believe that people should be allowed to enter into contracts and that when you enter into a contract you should be able to rely upon the agreement. In other words, people should be held to their promises.

*Warning: Do not sign a pre-nup or any other legal document that you do not understand or do not agree with. If you sign it, you are likely to be bound by it.*

Having said that, any party to a pre-nup can try to challenge it and can ask the Court to set it aside. The challenge would need to allege fraud, undue duress, overreaching, or that the pre-nup is extremely one sided to the point that it is unconscionable. Although these are ways that people challenge pre-nups, they are rarely, if ever, successful and in most cases the courts enforce the prenuptial agreements.

Here are some examples of pre-nup challenges. A person might claim that they did not sign it and that someone forged their name. If they did not sign it, they did not enter into the contract. There are handwriting experts that can be hired to prove whether the signature is valid. Someone might say they signed it, but their spouse drugged them so they did not know what they were doing. Or a person might say they signed it, but it was presented to them for the first time right before they walked down the aisle and they did not have time to read it or have a lawyer explain it.

*Best Practice: If you do not want to be held to it, do not sign it.*

Let's say you did sign a pre-nup and you have no good defense against it. Your spouse has filed for divorce. If he/she wants to hold you to the pre-nup and the pre-nup is clear about what happens in the event of divorce, it should simplify your divorce process. This is one of the benefits and reasons that people enter into prenuptial agreements. If neither one of you wants to follow the terms of the pre-nup, you can negotiate a different settlement.

*What if the pre-nup was crafted in another state? An out-of-state pre-nup does not affect the enforceability.*

# CHAPTER 13:

# LEGAL LIKELIHOODS

# IN TEXAS

> *Note: The law is ever changing and may have changed by the time you are reading this.*

## Sixty Day Waiting Period

In the state of Texas, there is a sixty day "waiting period" from the date the Petition for Divorce is filed to the date that you can finalize the divorce. This means that the quickest you can get divorced in Texas is sixty days. Technically, the Judge has the power to waive the sixty day waiting period, but would only do so in rare and unusual circumstances. As an example, one Judge in Collin County told us that he had never waived the waiting period after twenty years on the bench.

During the waiting period, we are not just waiting. We are working on reaching terms of divorce via settlement or judicial decision.

How likely is it that you can actually be done with this work and be ready to finalize your divorce at the end of the sixty day period? As of the writing of this book, the average case takes three to six months to finalize. Why does it take so long? There are a myriad of reasons, some of which are:

- The Court dockets are backed up in some counties and you cannot get a trial date more quickly than that.

- If you are handling your case collaboratively or trying to settle it using another method, it still takes a lot of time to gather all of the information for the professionals that are helping you. Once all of the information has been gathered, it takes time to review and evaluate the information, as well as develop settlement options.

- Sometimes one of the parties needs time to grieve the marriage and accept that they are divorcing before they can effectively move into the settlement phase.

# Child Support Formula & Issues

As of the writing of this book, child support is one of the clearest most predictable areas of the law. This is quite intentional because it is also one of the most enforceable areas of the law. The legislature wanted people to be crystal clear about what their obligation is before they can risk being imprisoned for failure to pay.

We advise that you ask your lawyer to calculate the amount for you because the law is ever changing. As of the writing of this book, let's say the child support payor (the one paying the child support) is named Pat. Please note that Pat, the payor, could be Mom or Dad. Pat would be ordered to pay child support based on a percentage of Pat's income.

There is no consideration of the other parent's income. We are going to call the other parent Alex, who again could be Mom or Dad. The percentage is based on how many children Pat has with Alex and how many children Pat has with someone other than Alex.

If Pat has no other children except for the children with Alex, then Pat would be ordered to pay 20 percent of his or her net pay (up to a cap) per month for the first child. If Pat and Alex have two children, it goes up to 25 percent. It continues to go up 5 percent per child until a maximum of 40 percent.

How does the income cap work? If Pat earns $8,550 or more net (after taxes and items required by law are withdrawn) per month, the percentage (20 to 40 percent depending on the number of children) is only applied to the first $8,550 of net income. Therefore, absent any proven special needs of the child, the most Pat could be Court ordered to pay for one child is $1,710 per month. Whether Pat earns $8,550 net per month or $75,000 net per month, the Court ordered child support is limited to $1,710 for one child.

Please note that, as mentioned earlier in the book, parents may agree to a child support amount that is different than what the Court ordered amount would be. This may occur in a collaborative process or other settlement process. When it happens, there are reasons and specific information that leads the parents to decide on a number that is most appropriate for their family situation.

# What is the Trend in Custody?

As of the writing of this book, we are seeing more and more parents with children ages eight and older decide to select an equal parenting time schedule which divides the time with the children fifty/fifty. Two popular 50/50 schedules are commonly referred to as "2/2/5/5" and "Week On / Week Off".

With a **2/2/5/5 schedule,** one parent (A) always has Monday and Tuesday from the time school gets out to the following morning. The other parent (B) always has Wednesday and Thursday from the time school gets out to the following morning. The weekends alternate between the parents. This creates periods with each parent of two days, two days, five days, five days, two days, etc.

## Example:

| SUN | MON | TUES | WED | THUR | FRI | SAT |
|-----|-----|------|-----|------|-----|-----|
| A | A | B | B | A | A | A |
| A | A | B | B | B | B | B |
| A | A | B | B | A | A | A |
| A | A | B | B | B | B | B |
| A | A | B | B | A | A | A |

## Week On / Week Off is exactly what it sounds like. One parent has
the children beginning when school gets out on Monday until school starts the following Monday. Then the other parent has the children from Monday after school until the next Monday morning. The weeks alternate.

## Example:

| SUN | MON | TUES | WED | THUR | FRI | SAT |
|-----|-----|------|-----|------|-----|-----|
| B | A | A | A | A | A | A |
| A | B | B | B | B | B | B |
| B | A | A | A | A | A | A |
| A | B | B | B | B | B | B |
| B | A | A | A | A | A | A |

The law in Texas still has a preference for a standard possession schedule (see **Appendix 7** for the standard possession schedule) where one parent has more time than the other. Therefore, Judges start from that premise and only adopt a 50/50 schedule if the facts of the case support equal parenting time over the presumption for the standard possession schedule.

As an example, let's say Parent "A" is the parent who will have less parenting time. Basically Parent "A" has the first, third and fifth weekends from Thursday after school until returning to school Monday morning. Every Thursday night is an overnight for Parent "A". Holidays basically alternate and Parent "A" has thirty days in the summer. Parent "B" has the rest of the time not awarded to Parent "A". Please note that this example is an over-simplification (see **Appendix 7** for details).

---

*A common deviation from the standard possession schedule is that parents often agree to a different summer arrangement.*

---

## Popular options include:

1. Maintaining the school year schedule during the summer except for a week or two with each parent for vacation.
2. Alternating weeks in the summer only.

# Division of Property

Texas is not an automatic 50/50 division state. The law states that the Judge should divide the community property in a fair and just manner. That generates several other questions such as: What is fair and just? Could it be 50/50? How likely is that? Does the judge divide each asset in half if the ruling is 50/50? Do we have to liquidate our estate in order to divide it 50/50? Do we have to pay penalties when our retirement is divided?

# CHAPTER 14:

# SUBSTANCE ABUSE

# & DIVORCE

Often, unhappy marriages lead to the use of substances as a means of coping.

Alcohol, illicit drugs and prescription drugs are coping mechanisms that individuals turn to when they are having difficulty with life and its many challenges.

Substance abuse at any time creates financial and relationship difficulties; however, during a divorce substance abuse can become a focal point that impacts many factors.

Undetected substance abuse can lead your spouse to believe that there may be mental health issues. Questions or accusations of mental health issues can lead to a request for a psychological evaluation. Psychological evaluations take time and can be expensive.

If a psychological evaluation is requested by your spouse or ordered by the Court, you will participate in a formal interview with a psychologist or psychiatrist. Along with that formal interview, you may be required to participate in the completion of assessment tests that can take hours to finish. Psychological evaluations assist the Court in determining if there are personality or behavior issues that impact a person's ability to act in their children's best interest.

If you believe that you or your spouse may have a substance abuse issue, it is important to be evaluated for the level of use/abuse. It is also important to have a defined treatment plan such as participation in a support program like Alcoholics Anonymous, Narcotics Anonymous or, if more serious, an outpatient or inpatient program.

If the Judge in your divorce case suspects substance abuse issues, they can order immediate participation in drug or alcohol testing. In addition, if substance abuse is determined to be present, the Judge could order a parent to wear an ankle bracelet or use a breathalyzer prior to parenting time.

> *It is critical that you do not pretend that you do not have a problem if you do. Also, do not take it lightly if you think your spouse may have a substance abuse problem.*

Get informed and talk to a trained third party to help determine if your concerns are reasonable. If the trained professional says that your spouse's behavior does not constitute substance abuse, let the issue go and move forward with the divorce process.

Evaluations can be completed by a Licensed Chemical Dependency Counselor (LCDC), as well as drug and alcohol treatment centers.

# CHAPTER 15:

# STRATEGIES

# FOR DEALING WITH

# A MENTALLY ILL SPOUSE

**Divorce is difficult with the best of circumstances, but the process of divorcing someone with a mental illness can be much more difficult.**

**As a rule of thumb, compassion is the best route to take; however, compassion without guilt is even better.**

Announcing the divorce to a mentally ill person may create a crisis that you and they will need support through. Unfortunately different mental illnesses may carry with them different reactions to the announcement that you want a divorce. Even when a mentally ill person's illness is being managed with medications, the announcement of divorce should be handled with great care. The stress related to divorce can increase mental illness characteristics.

Safety first is your first rule of thumb. If you believe that your spouse may react in a manner that is dangerous or threatening, please read the chapter earlier in this book about how to tell your spouse you want a divorce. Keep a record of conversations where you feel threatened as it may be useful if you need to file a restraining order.

Second, your spouse's reaction to your request for a divorce is not your fault or responsibility. It is not your fault if they choose to hurt themselves after you tell him/her you want a divorce. Your responsibility is how you react to his/her threats of "what they will do if you do not stay." Keep in mind that choosing to remain a hostage in your marriage out of fear of what he/she might do will not make things better.

Third, until the divorce is final, you may still be the person that has to make decisions for your spouse in regards to treatment. If there are minor children involved, do not be surprised if the Court relies heavily on information provided by court appointed professionals and/or your spouse's therapist/psychiatrist. In many states, courts will do all they can to award physical and legal custody to both parents equally unless one of the parents shows that the other parent poses a risk to the children. And in many cases the Court may still order supervised visitation.

*If you are dealing with a mentally ill spouse, find support for yourself through organizations such as the National Alliance on Mental Illness.*

# CHAPTER 16:

# STRATEGIES
# FOR DEALING
# WITH A SPOUSE
# COMING OUT OF
# THE CLOSET

In recent years, we have seen a greater frequency of divorce cases where one spouse is coming out of the closet.

When this happens, it is not unusual for it to be in a very long marriage and/or a very religious family.

Whether you are the straight spouse or the spouse coming out, the divorce process will be difficult, but can be manageable with the appropriate information and support.

If you are the straight spouse, it is important to know that **IT IS NOT YOUR FAULT!** You did not make your spouse gay. Hearing that may be enough to help you with your spouse's coming out and your pending divorce. It is normal to experience a lot of difficult feelings such as confusion, feeling rejected, being lied to, shame, guilt, worrying that you caused it, worrying about the children, embarrassment, betrayal, extreme anger, and questioning everything about your marriage. If these worries and feelings begin to affect your day-to-day living in a negative manner, you should seek the help of a therapist and a support group such as the Straight Spouse Network.

If you and your spouse have children, it will be important for them to have a therapist as well. Your children will be going through many similar emotional issues such as confusion, being lied to, shame, embarrassment, strong feelings of anger, what this means for their sexuality, what this means for their religious beliefs, etc. They will be experiencing all of these emotions, but will be less equip to handle them on their own which is why a therapist will be so valuable. Also, it will be difficult enough for you to manage through your own emotions and you may not be able to provide the appropriate type or amount of support for your children when they need it.

As an added complication, your religious views may have a very strong impact on how you handle the news that your spouse is gay. You may have to reconcile your own personal views or the views of your church with this news about your family. Regardless of your religious views, it is important to handle the divorce in a manner that is respectful of your spouse as a human being, as a parent to your children, and as someone with whom you shared a portion of your life. In regards to the children, it will be important to follow the guidelines of the therapist that they are seeing. Ideally, your children should see the therapist long enough to have developed a counseling relationship with them prior to disclosing the news to them. It may not always work out to have the therapist in place in advance; however, the sooner the better.

---

*As in any case where your spouse may have had sexual relations with another person, you should get tested for HIV/AIDS. Even if your spouse says they have only had protected intercourse with someone else, you should get tested for your own piece of mind and well-being.*

---

All future relationships with other romantic partners, whether heterosexual or homosexual, should be handled with care in regards to introducing your children. The length of the relationship and the seriousness of the relationship should drive whether or not the children are introduced. If your children are still seeing their therapist, it is important to discuss your desire to introduce the children with the therapist prior to introducing them.

# CHAPTER 17:

# WARNINGS

# Legal Separation in Texas

There is no such thing as legal separation in Texas. The closest thing that we have is a temporary order while you are divorcing. Or in a collaborative case you might reach agreements early in the process concerning interim issues such as who is going to live where while the divorce is pending, what the schedule will be with the children while the divorce is pending, and who will pay what bill while the divorce is pending.

# You Are Married Until You Are Divorced

Technically, from a legal perspective you are either married or divorced in Texas. There is no "legal separation". And therefore adultery is adultery regardless of whether it occurs two years before your divorce is final or the day before your divorce is final.

The main reason that it is advisable to refrain from relationships while you are still married (besides the moral and ethical considerations) is not because of the possible reaction from the Judge or jury, but because it will enrage your spouse and cause your case to become much more expensive financially and emotionally for your family. If you have children, it will make it much more difficult to co-parent post-divorce and much harder for your soon to be ex-spouse to accept the new person in your children's lives if the new person is viewed as the "home wrecker."

# Text Messages

Be aware that lawyers can always get records of the phone numbers that someone is texting, and sometimes can obtain the text messages themselves.

# Phone Records

Texting, calling, Facetime…the best way to find out if someone is having an affair is by pulling his or her phone records. People who are having affairs talk a lot and send a lot of text messages. They also tend to talk and text at strange hours and on holidays.

**114**

# Information You Do Not Want Your Spouse to Find

If you send data into the universe or store it on your cell phone, iPad or computer, there is always a risk that someone will find it or be able to restore it. It is very difficult to truly delete something.

As an example, Sam opened secret accounts in the Bahamas. He was moving community monies to these accounts to hide it from his wife Liz. Sam had records that would prove this on his computer at home. Liz's lawyer subpoenaed his hard drive. Before turning it over to comply with the subpoena, Sam erased the hard drive or erased the information about the accounts. Liz took it to a forensic computer expert and they were able to restore 95 percent of the information. Now Sam was in trouble for having the hidden accounts and for destroying evidence. Liz was smart because she obtained the computer quickly after the deleting occurred. The more time and work done on the computer after the deleting, the lower the chances are of recovering data.

# Toll Tag Records

It is possible to subpoena toll tag records which show the exact date and time that a car went through a specific toll booth.

As an example, Jessica claims that she is not having an affair with Ryan, but her husband Jeff thinks that she is. Jeff's lawyer subpoenas her toll tag records. Ryan lives near Exit 4 on the Tollway. The toll tag records show that Jessica is regularly going through that tollbooth late at night or early in the morning or when Jeff is out of town on business. Jessica has no other explanation for being in that part of town during those hours.

# Recording Laws in Texas

Some types of recording are legal and some are considered wiretapping which is highly illegal and considered a federal offense. It is important to be clear about the difference.

In Texas, it is legal to record a conversation as long as you are a party to it. In other words, if Jane is on the phone talking with her spouse John, she can record the conversation legally and play that recording for the Judge. She does not have a legal duty to inform John that she is recording the conversation as long as he knows that she is a party to the call.

On the other hand, if John is talking to his mistress on the phone in the house and Jane picks up another extension and listens in and records the conversation, this is highly illegal because John and his mistress did not know that Jane was on the phone.

As another example, let's say John and Jane are talking in person and Jane has a recording device in her pocket and she records John calling her ugly names and cursing at her. This is legal and she can play the recording for the Judge.

Alternatively, let's say Jane puts a recording device in John's car under the seat and John does not know it is there. She records him talking to his mistress in the car. This is highly illegal. Jane cannot play this for the Judge and, in fact, Jane could be federally prosecuted for illegal wiretapping.

# Assume Your Photo is Being Taken

One good rule of thumb when you are going through a divorce is to assume that the other lawyer has hired a private investigator to follow you and take your photograph. And also be aware that the Judge or jury will believe that where there is smoke there is fire.

Therefore, Leslie should not risk a photo being taken of her coming out of Jake's house at 2:00 a.m. Even though Jake is just a friend and she was just crying on his shoulder and nothing romantic happened. If her husband Chris or a Judge or jury sees a photo of Leslie coming out of Jake's house at 2:00 a.m., they WILL conclude that she is having an affair with Jake. That is enough proof. Fred does not have to obtain a photo of Leslie and Jake "in the act" for the Judge and jury to conclude that in fact adultery has occurred.

# False Allegations

On occasion, someone will make a false allegation to gain leverage or improve their position in the divorce case. For example, Elizabeth may lie and say that she thinks her husband Sebastian has sexually assaulted their 3-year old child. She may tell that lie thinking it will help her win the custody fight. Besides the obvious moral and ethical problems with this, most lies are found out. In other words, making a false allegation almost always backfires on the person telling the lie.

# The Internet as a Source of Information

You cannot believe everything you read on the Internet. The Internet is a wonderful resource, but be aware that there is no gate keeper screening who is posting out there. Articles, websites, blog posts, comments, and self-proclaimed "experts" may be accurate or may not. Also, when it comes to divorce, every state has different laws and laws can change over time.

Always trust your lawyer's advice over something you read on the Internet or over something your neighbor told you about their divorce. No two cases are identical.

# Using the Internet to Share Information

Be careful of your use of Facebook, Twitter, MySpace, Instagram, and other social media websites. When you are divorcing and your spouse thinks you are having an affair, not only will your spouse be looking at your social media accounts, but so will your spouse's friends, attorney, and maybe others. In some instances, it is not your social media page that is an issue, but it is your girlfriend's or boyfriend's page.

> *First piece of advice,*
> *do not have a girlfriend or boyfriend until after you are divorced.*

> *Second piece of advice,*
> *if it is too late for the first piece of advice,*
> *tell your girlfriend or boyfriend not to post photos*
> *of you or your children on his or her page.*

As an example, let's assume Drew and Cassidy are divorcing and have a baby named Chloe. Drew is having an affair with Kelsey. Kelsey posts a photo of herself with Drew and baby Chloe on her social media page where her nickname is "BlondBombShell". She also posts something rude about Cassidy on the site. Cassidy's friends discover this, print out the page and show it to Cassidy. Cassidy gives it to her lawyer. Her lawyer files a motion for an injunction asking the Court to require Kelsey, the BlondBombShell, to remove the photo of the child from the website and prohibiting her from posting any photos of the child in the future. Cassidy believes it can be unsafe to post photos of children on the internet, especially in Kelsey's circles. The Judge agrees and orders Kelsey to take down the photos. Unfortunately for Drew, this is the first hearing in his case and the first impression that the Court has of him. It is not a positive first impression and he did not even know that Kelsey was posting this on the Internet. He certainly did not give her permission to do so.

# Computers and Privacy

When is it a breach to hack into your spouse's computer? This is an unclear and complicated area of law. There is not a specific answer, but here is some general guidance. The Court is measuring the level to which a husband or wife had an expectation of privacy.

As an example, let's say husband's computer is at his office away from the home and is password protected. Wife does not have keys to the office and does not know his password. In this situation, it would definitely be a violation of law for her to access that computer data.

On the other hand, if husband's computer is the home computer, multiple family members use it and it is not password protected, any information on that computer would likely be legitimately acquired. Husband really had no expectation of privacy in that example.

You can see that there could be various other situations that fall between these two examples. Perhaps it is not the home computer, but husband brings his laptop home every night and it is not password protected and from time to time a family member uses it. That scenario could probably go either way.

# Change Your Passwords

It is very common during a divorce for spouses to try to read each other's emails and to try to monitor each other's banking and credit card use online. One problem this creates is that each person is probably having confidential communications with their lawyer via email.

It is important to change your passwords to new passwords that your spouse would never guess. Most people know the common passwords used by their spouse. Do not use those. Come up with a password that he or she would never dream of and that has nothing to do with you.

# Do Not Be Stupid

There are many things

that we consider to be common sense;

however, here are some important reminders.

- Resolution of your issues is easier when you treat each other with respect.

- Do not call your girlfriend or boyfriend in the midst of a collaborative meeting with your spouse, both attorneys, the financial professional and the mental health professional.

- Do not unexpectedly change how or where your paycheck is deposited.

- Do not bring your girlfriend or boyfriend to your child's athletic events while you are still married.

- Do not have your girlfriend or boyfriend around your children at all during the divorce and for a reasonable period after the divorce is final.

- Do not show the divorce pleadings to your child.

- Do not start charging a lot of excessive expenses on your spouse's credit card right before the divorce is final.

- Do not start calling your spouse by their first name to your children. It will hurt the children and make your spouse mad.

- Do not say anything bad about your spouse to your child. Not because it hurts your spouse, but because it hurts your child. On a very basic level, your children see themselves as one half Mom and one half Dad. When something bad is said about their other parent they personalize that to mean that THEY are also that way. Doing this is a personal attack on your child's self esteem and it can cause them to see themselves negatively. This includes telling your children that the other parent is making you move, that there is not enough money because of your spouse, that your spouse had an affair. Sometimes people justify telling their children these things because it is "the truth". We withhold the truth from our children about many things as they grow up in an effort to protect them. This is a time when it is more important to protect them than to tell them "the truth." Also, "the truth" is most likely different for you and your spouse.

# CHAPTER 18:

# MYTHS ABOUT DIVORCE

## Myth: If you leave the house, you will be accused of abandonment.

If you move out of the house at the time of filing for divorce or within a few months of the filing for divorce that does not qualify as abandonment. You also are not waiving or losing your interest in a portion of the equity by moving out of the house.

## Myth: Your spouse will be crucified by the Judge for his or her affair.

The truth is that judges do not like affairs and certainly there is some legal significance as to how they can affect your estate division and custody case. However, many spouses are disappointed because they do not think that the punishment meets the crime from their perspective.

Judges are not gasping and looking with condemnation at the cheater. They hear about affairs day after day, case after case. A significant number of divorce cases involve one person having an affair and, although it is a very identifiable betrayal, it is usually not the only betrayal in the relationship and is typically a symptom of a failed marriage rather than the cause of it.

People who are happily married in a healthy marriage typically do not cheat. Courts have an understanding that most likely both parties are to blame for the failure of the marriage (even if it is not in equal parts).

## Myth: Drug use will cause termination of parental access.

Of course judges do not like drug use when children are involved. However, they do not terminate or eliminate a parent from the child's life because they are using drugs. If a party tests positive for drugs or admits to using drugs, but they are on a path to sobriety (such as rehab, Alcoholics Anonymous®, or other positive steps), the judges will keep these parents in the children's lives with the goal being to regain a normal parent-child relationship. There may be supervision for that parent at first, depending on the circumstances, to keep the children safe while the parent proves their sincerity in getting clean and sober. It is much better to admit to a problem and seek help than to deny it.

# Myth: I'll get my day in court OR I need my day in court.

What people want when they say this is for the Judge to hear the whole story and to really understand the situation. And if the Judge were to hear the whole story, they assume that it would certainly turn out favorably. The problems:

1.      **Time Limitations:** The Courts are busy. Judges do not have time to learn every detail of your twenty-year marriage.

2.      **Rules of Evidence:** Only certain parts of the story will be allowed to be told because of the rules of evidence. There are very specific rules that determine what can and cannot be presented to the Judge or Jury. For example, no one can write a letter or sign an affidavit and send it to the Judge or have you present it to the Judge. Witnesses must appear in person. It is not always feasible to get Cousin Fred from Ohio to the Court to testify. If Fred cannot come in person, he cannot send a written statement, except in very limited circumstances.

3.      **Postponements:** It may take a very long time to get to trial, especially in counties where the Judge also hears criminal cases. Criminal cases take priority under the law. Therefore, your divorce case may be set to be heard on Wednesday and we are all there and ready to put on our case, but the Judge tells us we have to come back in 3 months because the docket is too full or because a criminal case took priority.

# Myth: The courts favor mothers for primary custody.

Under the law, the courts are no longer allowed to discriminate based upon the gender of the parent. In practicality, Judges favor the parent that has been most involved historically with the day-to-day physical care of the child.

# The top eight threats made during divorce cases.

1. I will take the children.

2. I will withhold the children from you.

3. I will take the money.

4. I will tell everyone the bad facts about you (the other parent).

5. I will not allow our child to participate in certain activities in which you (the other parent) want the child to participate.

6. I will fight you to the end.

7. I will quit working to avoid paying child support.

8. If you leave me, I will hurt myself or hurt you.

# It is best for your case not to make threats.

If you are the one receiving the threats, please remember that your spouse does not control many of these decisions. Just because she or he says something, it does not make their statement true. Unless you are an axe murderer (or something similarly horrible), your spouse cannot "take the children" from you.

A judge will give you specific times that are your exclusive times with your children. If your ex-spouse tries to interfere, the Judge can put him or her in jail. If someone quits their job to avoid paying child support, the Court can, and likely will, assume that they still have the job when setting the child support amount. Do not be intimidated by these threats. That is the reason your spouse is making them – to intimidate you.

> *Know that the Judge has much*
> *more power than your spouse.*

# CHAPTER 19:

# HAPPY ENDINGS

The purpose of this book is to help inform you about what to expect during the divorce process and tips for making it a better experience for you, your spouse and your children.

While divorce is generally seen as a negative event, there are positive things about it and it can bring hope for a better tomorrow.

We are in no way encouraging or promoting divorce.

It should always be a last resort after trying to find other ways to resolve the problems in your marriage.

However, many couples do eventually divorce and it is important to be informed.

# Here are a few benefits
# you may find following a divorce:

- You will not spend so much time being angry and upset. You will become a happier person.

- You will not have to argue all the time or argue in front of your children.

- You will develop a greater appreciation for time with your children because there will be periods when they are with their other parent.

- You will get "breaks" from parenting which will allow you to become a better parent.

- You will have more freedom and be able to make your own decisions. You can reconnect with who you truly are.

- You can eventually find a partner who loves you and respects you, someone with whom you can have fun and who can become your best friend.

- You can develop a great co-parenting relationship with your children's other parent.

We know how hard it is to make the decision to divorce and how hard the process can be. It is our hope that you will utilize the resources available to you and choose to take the high road during the process. We hope that you will always try to do what is best for children, even when it is difficult.

---

*We hope that you will become the model for how people can go through a divorce in a respectful way, create a better life for themselves, and become great co-parents for their children.*

---

# APPENDIX 1

## Children's Bill of Rights

*We commit to this parenting plan with the mutual goals of doing what is best for our children and minimizing the negative effects of conflict on him/her.*

*We will take steps to assure that our children have frequent and continuing contact with both of us.*

*We will encourage and accept a positive relationship between our children and us.*

*We will be respectful of each other.*

*We will create an environment in which our children will not feel their loyalties to us are torn.*

*We pledge to provide a safe and stable environment for our children.*


*We believe our children's physical, psychological, emotional and financial needs will benefit from the implementation of our parenting plan.*


*We recognize the need to provide for our children's changing needs as they grow and mature.*


*We recognize the value of having a clear and understandable agreement to share our parenting responsibilities.*

# Our children are entitled
# to enjoy the following rights:

1. The right to be treated as an important human being, with unique feelings, ideas and desires and not as a source of argument between parents.

2. The right to a sense of security and belonging derived from a loving and nurturing environment which shelters them from harm.

3. The right to a continuing relationship with both parents and the freedom to receive love from and express love for both.

4. The right to parents who will listen to and show respect for what their child has to say.

5. The right to express love and affection for each parent without having to stifle that love because of fear of disapproval by the other parent.

6. The right to grow and flourish in an atmosphere free of exploitation, abuse and neglect.

7. The right to know their parents' decision to divorce is not their responsibility and they will still be able to live with each parent.

8. The right to continuing care and guidance from both parents where they can be educated in mind, nourished in spirit, and developed in body, in an environment of unconditional love.

9. The right to receive developmentally appropriate answers to questions about changing family relationships.

10. The right to know and appreciate what is good in each parent without one parent degrading the other.

11. The right to have a relaxed, secure relationship with both parents without being placed in a position to manipulate one parent against the other.

12. The right to have one parent not undermine time with the other parent by suggesting tempting alternatives or by threatening to withhold activities with the other parent as a punishment for the child's wrongdoing.

13. The right to be able to experience regular and consistent parental contact and the right to know, in a developmentally appropriate manner, the reason for not having regular contact.

14. The right to be a child and to be insulated from the conflict and problems of parents.

15. The right to be taught, according to developmental levels, to understand values, to assume responsibility for their actions, and to cope with the just consequences of their choices.

16. The right to be able to participate in their own destiny.

17. The right not to be used as a messenger between parents.

---

*We promise to give our children better protection*
*than any law could ever provide.*

# APPENDIX 2

# Children in the Middle's Rules for Co-Parenting

1. Do not talk negatively, or allow others to talk negatively, about the other parent, their family and friends, or their home in hearing range of the child. This would include belittling remarks, ridicules, or bringing up allegations that are valid or invalid about adult issues.

2. Do not question the children about the other parent or the activities of the other parent regarding their personal lives. In specific terms, do not use the child to spy on the other parent.

3. Do not argue or have heated conversations when the children are present or during exchanges.

4. Do not make promises to the children to try and win them over at the expense of the other parent.

5. Do communicate with the other parent and make similar rules in reference to discipline, routines, sleeping arrangements, and schedules. Appropriate discipline should be exercised by mutually agreed upon adults.

6. At all times, the decisions made by the parents will be for the child's psychological, spiritual, and physical wellbeing and safety.

7. Parenting time arrangements will be made and confirmed beforehand between the parents without involving the child.

8. Do notify each other in a timely manner of need to deviate from the order including canceling time with the child, rescheduling, and promptness.

9.  Do not schedule activities for the child during the other parent's time with the children without the other parent's consent. However we will work together to allow the child to be involved in extracurricular activities.

10. Do keep the other parent informed of any scholastic, medical, psychiatric, or extracurricular activities or appointments of the child.

11. Do keep the other parent informed at all times of your address and telephone number. If you are out of town with the child, do provide the other parent the address and phone where the children may be reached in case of an emergency.

12. Do refer to the other parent as the child's "mother" or "father" in conversation, rather than using the parent's first name, last name, or "my ex".

13. Do not bring the child into adult issues and conversations about custody, the court, or about the other party.

14. Do not ask the child where he or she wants to live.

15. Do not attempt to alienate the other parent from the child's life.

16. Do not allow stepparents or others to negatively alter or modify your relationship with the other parent.

17. Do not use phrases that draw the children into your issues or make the children feel guilty about the time spent with the other parent. Do not say, "I miss you." Do say "I love you."

# APPENDIX 3
## Online Co-Parenting Classes

www.ChildrenintheMiddle.com

www.ChildSharing.com

www.PuttingKidsFirst.org

www.OnlineParentClass.com

www.ParentingPartnerships.com

www.MakingTwoHomesWork.com

# APPENDIX 4
## Co-Parenting Support Tools

www.OurFamilyWizard.com

www.ShareKids.com

www.Rainbows.org

www.ParentingPartnerships.com

# APPENDIX 5
## Domestic Violence Resources in North Texas

National Domestic Violence Hotline at 1.800.799.SAFE(7233)

Adult & Child Abuse Hotline    1.800.252.5400

Al-Anon  & Alateen   214.363.0461

Alcoholics Anonymous  972.239.4599

Catholic Charities (Immigration issues)  214.946.4889

Central Dallas Ministries  214.823.8766

Contact Dallas  972.233.2233

Family Violence Legal Line  1.800.374.HOPE

Information & Referral  214.379.4357 or 211

Legal Services of North Texas  214.748.1234

Rape Crisis Center  214.590.0430

Suicide Crisis Center  214.824.7020

Police Dept. Family Violence Counselor  214.671.4304

Shelter: Brighter Tomorrows  972.262.8383

Shelter: Dallas County-Genesis Shelter  214.942.2998

Shelter: Dallas County-Mosaic Family Services  214.823.4434

Shelter: Dallas County-New Beginnings  972.276.0057

Shelter: Dallas County-Salvation Army  214.424.7208

Shelter: Dallas County-The Family Place  214.941.1991

Shelter: Collin County-Hope's Door  972.422.7233

Shelter: Denton County Friends of the Family  800.572.4031

Shelter: Tarrant County-Safe Haven  877.701.7233

# APPENDIX 6

# Dallas County's Standing Order
# This gives you an idea of the typical contents.

AMENDED DALLAS COUNTY FAMILY DISTRICT COURTS
GENERAL ORDERS
(Revised November 1, 2007)

DALLAS COUNTY STANDING ORDER REGARDING CHILDREN,
PETS, PROPERTY AND CONDUCT OF THE PARTIES

No party to this lawsuit has requested this order. Rather, this order is a standing order of the Dallas County District Courts that applies in every divorce suit and every suit affecting the parent-child relationship filed in Dallas County. The District Court of Dallas County giving preference to family law matters have adopted this order because the parties, their children and the family pets should be protected and their property preserved while the lawsuit is pending before the court.
Therefore, it is ORDERED:

1.       NO DISRUPTION OF CHILDREN. Both parties are ORDERED to refrain from doing the following acts concerning any children who are subjects of this case:
1.1.       Removing the children from the State of Texas, acting directly or in concert with others, without the written agreement of both parties or an order of this Court.
1.2.       Disrupting or withdrawing the children from the school or day-care facility where the children are presently enrolled, without the written agreement of both parents or an order of this Court.
1.3.       Hiding or secreting the children from the other parent or changing the children's current place of abode, without the written agreement of both parents or an order of this Court.
1.4.       Disturbing the peace of the children.
1.5.       Making disparaging remarks regarding the other party in the presence or within the hearing of the children.

2.       PROTECTION OF FAMILY PETS OR COMPANION ANIMALS. Both parties are to refrain from harming, threatening, interfering with the care, custody, or control of a pet, companion animal, that is possessed by a person protected by this order or by a member of the family or household of a person protected by this order.

3.       CONDUCT OF THE PARTIES DURING THE CASE.       Both parties are ORDERED to refrain from doing the following acts:
3.1.       Using vulgar, profane, obscene, or indecent language, or a coarse or offensive manner to communicate with the other party, whether in person, by telephone, or in writing.

3.2.     Threatening the other party in person, by telephone, or in writing to take unlawful action against any person.

3.3.     Placing one or more telephone calls, at an unreasonable hour, in an offensive or repetitious manner, without a legitimate purpose of communication, or anonymously.

4.     PRESERVATION OF PROPERTY AND USE OF FUNDS DURING DIVORCE CASE.  If this is a divorce case, both parties to the marriage are ORDERED to refrain from doing the following acts:

4.1.     Destroying, removing, concealing, encumbering, transferring, or otherwise harming or reducing the value of the property of one or both of the parties.

4.2.     Misrepresenting or refusing to disclose to the other party or to the Court, on proper request, the existence, amount, or location of any property of one or both of the parties.

4.3.     Damaging or destroying the tangible property of one or both of the parties, including any document that represents or embodies anything of value, and causing pecuniary loss to the other party.

4.4.     Tampering with the tangible property of one or both of the parties, including any document that represents or embodies anything of value, and causing pecuniary loss to the other party.

4.5.     Selling, transferring, assigning, mortgaging, encumbering, or in any other manner alienating any of the property of either party, whether personal property or real estate property, and whether separate or community, except as specifically authorized by this order.

4.6.     Incurring any indebtedness, other than legal expenses in connection with this suit, except as specifically authorized by this order.

4.7.     Making withdrawals from any checking or savings account in any financial institution for any purpose, except as specifically authorized by this order.

4.8.     Spending any sum of cash in either party's possession or subject to either party's control for any purpose, except as specifically authorized by this order.

4.9.     Withdrawing or borrowing in any manner for any purpose from any retirement, profit-sharing, pension, death, or other employee benefit plan or employee savings plan or from any individual retirement account or Keogh account, except as specifically authorized by this order.

4.10.     Signing or endorsing the other party's name on any negotiable instrument, check, or draft, such as tax refunds, insurance payments, and dividends, or attempting to negotiate any negotiable instrument payable to the other party without the personal signature of the other party.

4.11.     Taking any action to terminate or limit credit or charge cards in the name of the other party.

4.12.     Entering, operating, or exercising control over the motor vehicle in the possession of the other party.

4.13.     Discontinuing or reducing the withholding for federal income taxes on wages or salary while this suit is pending.

4.14.     Terminating or in any manner affecting the service of water, electricity, gas, telephone, cable television, or other contractual services, such as security, pest control, landscaping, or yard maintenance at the other party's residence or in any manner attempting to withdraw any deposits for service in connection with such services.

4.15.     Excluding the other party from the use and enjoyment of the other party's residence.

4.16.     Opening or redirecting the mail addressed to the other party.

5.    PERSONAL AND BUSINESS RECORDS IN DIVORCE CASE. "Records" means any tangible document or recording and includes e-mail or other digital or electronic data, whether stored on a computer hard drive, diskette or other electronic storage device. If this is a divorce case, both parties to the marriage are ORDERED to refrain from doing the following acts:
Concealing or destroying any family records, property records, financial records, business records or any records of income, debts, or other obligations.
Falsifying any writing or record relating to the property of either party.

INSURANCE IN DIVORCE CASE. If this is a divorce case, both parties to the marriage are ORDERED to refrain from doing the following acts:
Withdrawing or borrowing in any manner all or any part of the cash surrender value of life insurance policies on the life of either party, except as specifically authorized by this order.
Changing or in any manner altering the beneficiary designation on any life insurance on the life of either party or the parties' children.
Canceling, altering, or in any manner affecting any casualty, automobile, or health insurance policies insuring the parties' property of persons including the parties' minor children.

SPECIFIC AUTHORIZATIONS IN DIVORCE CASE. If this is a divorce case, both parties to the marriage are specifically authorized to do the following:
To engage in acts reasonable and necessary to the conduct of that party's usual business and occupation.
To make expenditures and incur indebtedness for reasonable attorney's fees and expenses in connection with this suit.
To make expenditures and incur indebtedness for reasonable and necessary living expenses for food, clothing, shelter, transportation and medical care.
To make withdrawals from accounts in financial institutions only for the purpose authorized by this order.

SERVICE AND APPLICATION OF THIS ORDER.
The Petitioner shall attach a copy of this order to the original petition and to each copy of the petition. At the time the petition is filed, if the Petitioner has failed to attach a copy of this order to the petition and any copy of the petition, the Clerk shall ensure that a copy of this order is attached to the petition and every copy of the petition presented.
This order is effective upon the filing of the original petitioner and shall remain in full force and effect as a temporary restraining order for fourteen days after the date of the filing of the original petition. If no party contests this order by presenting evidence at a hearing on or before fourteen days after the date of the filing of the original petition, this order shall continue in full force and effect as a temporary injunction until further order of the court. This entire order will terminate and will no longer be effective once the court signs a final order.

EFFECT OF OTHER COURT ORDERS. If any part of this order is different from any part of a protective order that has already been entered or is later entered, the protective order provisions prevail. Any part of this order not changed by some later order remains in full force and effect until the court signs a final decree.

PARTIES ENCOURAGED TO MEDIATE. The parties are encouraged to settle their disputes amicably without court intervention. The parties are encouraged to use alternative dispute resolution methods, such as mediation or informal settlement conferences (if appropriate), to resolve the conflicts that may arise in this lawsuit.

BOND WAIVED. It is ORDERED that the requirement of a bond is waived.

THIS DALLAS COUNTY AMENDED STANDING ORDER REGARDING CHILDREN, PROPERTY AND COUNDUCT OF THE PARTIES SHALL BECOME EFFECTIVE ON OCTOBER 8, 2007.


_____
HONORABLE JAMES MARTIN
254th District Court

_____
HONORABLE TENA CALLAHAN
302nd District Court


_____
HONORABLE LORI HOCKETT
255th District Court

_____
HONORABLE DENNISE GARCIA
303rd District Court


_____
HONORABLE DAVID LOPEZ
256th District Court

_____
HONORABLE ANDREA PLUMLEE
330th District Court


_____
HONORABLE LYNN CHERRY
301st District Court

# APPENDIX 7
## Standard Possession Order

The Court finds that the following provisions of this Standard Possession Order are intended to and do comply with the requirements of Texas Family Code sections 153.311 through 153.317. IT IS ORDERED that each conservator shall comply with all terms and conditions of this Standard Possession Order. IT IS ORDERED that this Standard Possession Order is effective immediately and applies to all periods of possession occurring on and after the date the Court signs this Standard Possession Order. IT IS, THEREFORE, ORDERED:

(a)      Definitions

     1.      In this Standard Possession Order "school" means the primary or secondary school in which the child is enrolled or, if the child is not enrolled in a primary or secondary school, the public school district in which the child primarily resides.

     2.      In this Standard Possession Order "child" includes each child, whether one or more, who is a subject of this suit while that child is under the age of eighteen years and not otherwise emancipated.

(b)      Mutual Agreement or Specified Terms for Possession

     IT IS ORDERED that the conservators shall have possession of the child at times mutually agreed to in advance by the parties, and, in the absence of mutual agreement, it is ORDERED that the conservators shall have possession of the child under the specified terms set out in this Standard Possession Order.

(c)      Parents Who Reside 100 Miles or Less Apart

     Except as otherwise explicitly provided in this Standard Possession Order, when Parent B resides 100 miles or less from the primary residence of the child, Parent B shall have the right to possession of the child as follows:

     1.      Weekends—

     On weekends that occur during the regular school term, beginning at [select one: 6:00 P.M./the time the child's school is regularly dismissed/or specify other time elected between school dismissal and 6:00 P.M.] on the first, third, and fifth Friday of each month and ending at [select one: 6:00 P.M. on the following Sunday/the time the child's school resumes after the weekend].

On weekends that do not occur during the regular school term, beginning at 6:00 P.M. on the first, third, and fifth Friday of each month and ending at 6:00 P.M. on the following Sunday.

2. Weekend Possession Extended by a Holiday—Except as otherwise explicitly provided in this Standard Possession Order, if a weekend period of possession by Parent B begins on a Friday that is a school holiday during the regular school term or a federal, state, or local holiday during the summer months when school is not in session, or if the period ends on or is immediately followed by a Monday that is such a holiday, that weekend period of possession shall begin at [select one: 6:00 P.M./the time the child's school is regularly dismissed/or specify other time elected between school dismissal and 6:00 P.M.] on the Thursday immediately preceding the Friday holiday or school holiday or end [select one: at 6:00 P.M. on that Monday holiday or school holiday/at 6:00 P.M. on that Monday holiday or at the time school resumes after that school holiday], as applicable.

3. Thursdays—On Thursday of each week during the regular school term, beginning at [select one: 6:00 P.M./the time the child's school is regularly dismissed/or specify other time elected between school dismissal and 6:00 P.M.] and ending at [select one: 8:00 P.M./the time the child's school resumes on Friday].

4. Spring Break in Even-Numbered Years—In even-numbered years, beginning at [select one: 6:00 P.M./the time the child's school is regularly dismissed/or specify other time elected between school dismissal and 6:00 P.M.] on the day the child is dismissed from school for the school's spring vacation and ending at [select one: 6:00 P.M. on the day before/the time] school resumes after that vacation.

5. Extended Summer Possession by Parent B—

With Written Notice by April 1—If Parent B gives Parent A written notice by April 1 of a year specifying an extended period or periods of summer possession for that year, Parent B shall have possession of the child for thirty days beginning no earlier than the day after the child's school is dismissed for the summer vacation and ending no later than seven days before school resumes at the end of the summer vacation in that year, to be exercised in no more than two separate periods of at least seven consecutive days each, as specified in the written notice [include if applicable: , provided that the period or periods of extended summer possession do not interfere with Father's Day Weekend]. These periods of possession shall begin and end at 6:00 P.M.

Without Written Notice by April 1—If Parent B does not give Parent A written notice by April 1 of a year specifying an extended period or periods of summer possession for that year, Parent B shall have possession of the child for thirty consecutive days in that year beginning at 6:00 P.M. on July 1 and ending at 6:00 P.M. on July 31.

Notwithstanding the Thursday periods of possession during the regular school term and the weekend periods of possession ORDERED for Parent B, it is explicitly ORDERED that Parent A shall have a superior right of possession of the child as follows:

      1.      Spring Break in Odd–Numbered Years—In odd-numbered years, beginning at 6:00 P.M. on the day the child is dismissed from school for the school's spring vacation and ending at 6:00 P.M. on the day before school resumes after that vacation.

      2.      Summer Weekend Possession by Sole Managing Conservator—If Parent A gives Parent B written notice by April 15 of a year, Parent A shall have possession of the child on any one weekend beginning at 6:00 P.M. on Friday and ending at 6:00 P.M. on the following Sunday during any one period of the extended summer possession by Parent B in that year, provided that Parent A picks up the child from Parent B and returns the child to that same place [include if applicable: and that the weekend so designated does not interfere with Father's Day Weekend].

      3.      Extended Summer Possession by Sole Managing Conservator—If Parent A gives Parent B written notice by April 15 of a year or gives Parent B fourteen days' written notice on or after April 16 of a year, Parent A may designate one weekend beginning no earlier than the day after the child's school is dismissed for the summer vacation and ending no later than seven days before school resumes at the end of the summer vacation, during which an otherwise scheduled weekend period of possession by Parent B shall not take place in that year, provided that the weekend so designated does not interfere with Parent B's period or periods of extended summer possession [include if applicable: or with Father's Day Weekend].

(d)      Parents Who Reside More Than 100 Miles Apart

Except as otherwise explicitly provided in this Standard Possession Order, when Parent B resides more than 100 miles from the residence of the child, Parent B shall have the right to possession of the child as follows:

      1.      Weekends—Unless Parent B elects the alternative period of weekend possession described in the next paragraph, Parent B shall have the right to possession of the child on weekends that occur during the regular school term, beginning at [select one: 6:00 P.M./the time the child's school is regularly dismissed/or specify other time elected between school dismissal and 6:00 P.M.] on the first, third, and fifth Friday of each month and ending at [select one: 6:00 P.M. on the following Sunday/the time the child's school resumes after the weekend], and on weekends that do not occur during the regular school

term, beginning at 6:00 P.M. on the first, third, and fifth Friday of each month and ending at 6:00 P.M. on the following Sunday. Except as otherwise explicitly provided in this Standard Possession Order, if such a weekend period of possession by Parent B begins on a Friday that is a school holiday during the regular school term or a federal, state, or local holiday during the summer months when school is not in session, or if the period ends on or is immediately followed by a Monday that is such a holiday, that weekend period of possession shall begin at [select one: 6:00 P.M./the time the child's school is regularly dismissed/or specify other time elected between school dismissal and 6:00 P.M.] on the Thursday immediately preceding the Friday holiday or school holiday or end [select one: at 6:00 P.M. on that Monday holiday or school holiday/at 6:00 P.M. on that Monday holiday or at the time school resumes after that school holiday], as applicable.

[Or]

1.        Weekend—One weekend per month, of Parent B's choice, beginning at [select one: 6:00 P.M./the time the child's school is regularly dismissed/or specify other time elected between school dismissal and 6:00 P.M.] on the day school recesses for the weekend and ending at [select one: 6:00 P.M. on the day before school resumes/the time the child's school resumes] after the weekend, provided that Parent B gives Parent A fourteen days' written or telephonic notice preceding a designated weekend. The weekends chosen shall not conflict with the provisions regarding Christmas, Thanksgiving, the child's birthday, and [Father's/Mother's] Day Weekend below.

[Continue with the following]

2.        Spring Break in All Years—Every year, beginning at [select one: 6:00 P.M./the time the child's school is regularly dismissed/or specify other time elected between school dismissal and 6:00 P.M.] on the day the child is dismissed from school for the school's spring vacation and ending at [select one: 6:00 P.M. on the day before/the time] school resumes after that vacation.

3.        Extended Summer Possession by Parent B—

With Written Notice by April 1—If Parent B gives Parent A written notice by April 1 of a year specifying an extended period or periods of summer possession for that year, Parent B shall have possession of the child for forty-two days beginning no earlier than the day after the child's school is dismissed for the summer vacation and ending no later than seven days before school resumes at the end of the summer vacation in that year, to be exercised in no more than two separate periods of at least seven consecutive days each, as specified in the written notice [include if applicable: , provided that the period or periods of extended summer possession do not interfere with Father's Day Weekend]. These periods of possession shall begin and end at 6:00 P.M.

Notwithstanding the weekend periods of possession ORDERED for Parent B, it is explicitly ORDERED that Parent A shall have a superior right of possession of the child as follows:

1.      Summer Weekend Possession by Sole Managing Conservator—If Parent A gives Parent B written notice by April 15 of a year, Parent A shall have possession of the child on any one weekend beginning at 6:00 P.M. on Friday and ending at 6:00 P.M. on the following Sunday during any one period of possession by Parent B during Parent B's extended summer possession in that year, provided that if a period of possession by Parent B in that year exceeds thirty days, Parent A may have possession of the child under the terms of this provision on any two nonconsecutive weekends during that period and provided that Parent A picks up the child from Parent B and returns the child to that same place [include if applicable: and that the weekend so designated does not interfere with Father's Day Weekend].

2.      Extended Summer Possession by Sole Managing Conservator—If Parent A gives Parent B written notice by April 15 of a year, Parent A may designate twenty-one days beginning no earlier than the day after the child's school is dismissed for the summer vacation and ending no later than seven days before school resumes at the end of the summer vacation in that year, to be exercised in no more than two separate periods of at least seven consecutive days each, during which Parent B shall not have possession of the child, provided that the period or periods so designated do not interfere with Parent B's period or periods of extended summer possession [include if applicable: or with Father's Day Weekend].

(e)      Holidays Unaffected by Distance

Notwithstanding the weekend and Thursday periods of possession of Parent B, Parent A and Parent B shall have the right to possession of the child as follows:

1.      Christmas Holidays in Even-Numbered Years—In even-numbered years, Parent B shall have the right to possession of the child beginning at [select one: 6:00 P.M./the time the child's school is regularly dismissed/or specify other time elected between school dismissal and 6:00 P.M.] on the day the child is dismissed from school for the Christmas school vacation and ending at noon on December 28, and Parent A shall have the right to possession of the child beginning at noon on December 28 and ending at 6:00 P.M. on the day before school resumes after that Christmas school vacation.

2. Christmas Holidays in Odd-Numbered Years—In odd-numbered years, Parent A shall have the right to possession of the child beginning at 6:00 P.M. on the day the child is dismissed from school for the Christmas school vacation and ending at noon on December 28, and Parent B shall have the right to possession of the child beginning at noon on December 28 and ending at [select one: 6:00 P.M. on the day before/the time] the child's school resumes after that Christmas school vacation.

3. Thanksgiving in Odd-Numbered Years—In odd-numbered years, Parent B shall have the right to possession of the child beginning at [select one: 6:00 P.M./the time the child's school is regularly dismissed/or specify other time elected between school dismissal and 6:00 P.M.] on the day the child is dismissed from school for the Thanksgiving holiday and ending at [select one: 6:00 P.M. on the Sunday following Thanksgiving/the time the child's school resumes after that Thanksgiving holiday].

4. Thanksgiving in Even-Numbered Years—In even-numbered years, Parent A shall have the right to possession of the child beginning at 6:00 P.M. on the day the child is dismissed from school for the Thanksgiving holiday and ending at 6:00 P.M. on the Sunday following Thanksgiving.

5. Child's Birthday—If a conservator is not otherwise entitled under this Standard Possession Order to present possession of [the/a] child on the child's birthday, that conservator shall have possession of the child [include if desired: and the child's minor siblings] beginning at 6:00 P.M. and ending at 8:00 P.M. on that day, provided that that conservator picks up the child[ren] from the other conservator's residence and returns the child[ren] to that same place.

6. Father's Day Weekend—Father shall have the right to possession of the child each year, beginning at 6:00 P.M. on the Friday preceding Father's Day and ending at 6:00 P.M. on Father's Day, provided that if Father is not otherwise entitled under this Standard Possession Order to present possession of the child, he shall pick up the child from the other conservator's residence and return the child to that same place.

7. Mother's Day Weekend—Mother shall have the right to possession of the child each year, beginning at 6:00 P.M. on the Friday preceding Mother's Day and ending at 6:00 P.M. on Mother's Day, provided that if Mother is not otherwise entitled under this Standard Possession Order to present possession of the child, she shall pick up the child from the other conservator's residence and return the child to that same place.

(f)        Undesignated Periods of Possession

Parent A shall have the right of possession of the child at all other times not specifically designated in this Standard Possession Order for Parent B.

(g)        General Terms and Conditions

Except as otherwise explicitly provided in this Standard Possession Order, the terms and conditions of possession of the child that apply regardless of the distance between the residence of a parent and the child are as follows:

1.        Surrender of Child by Sole Managing Conservator—Parent A is ORDERED to surrender the child to Parent B at the beginning of each period of Parent B's possession at the residence of Sole Managing Conservator.

[Include the following language if applicable.]

If a period of possession by Parent B begins at the time the child's school is regularly dismissed, Parent A is ORDERED to surrender the child to Parent B at the beginning of each such period of possession at the school in which the child is enrolled. If the child is not in school, Parent B shall pick up the child at the residence of Parent A at [time], and Parent A is ORDERED to surrender the child to Parent B at the residence of Parent A at [time] under these circumstances.

[Select one of the following]

2.        Surrender of Child by Parent B—Parent B is ORDERED to surrender the child to Parent A at the residence of Parent B at the end of each period of possession.

[Or]

2.        Return of Child by Parent B—Parent B is ORDERED to return the child to the residence of Parent A at the end of each period of possession. However, it is ORDERED that, if Parent A and Parent B live in the same county at the time of rendition of this order, Parent B's county of residence remains the same after rendition of this order, and Sole Managing Conservator's county of residence changes, effective on the date of the change of residence by Sole Managing Conservator, Parent B shall surrender the child to Parent A at the residence of Parent B at the end of each period of possession.

[If alternate possession times are used for ending any period of possession (Texas Family Code 153.317), include the following paragraph.]

If a period of possession by Parent B ends at the time the child's school resumes, Parent B is ORDERED to surrender the child to Parent A at the end of each such period of possession at the school in which the child is enrolled or, if the child is not in school, at the residence of Parent A at [time].

[Continue with the following]

3.      Surrender of Child by Parent B—Parent B is ORDERED to surrender the child to Sole Managing Conservator, if the child is in Parent B's possession or subject to Parent B's control, at the beginning of each period of Sole Managing Conservator's exclusive periods of possession, at the place designated in this Standard Possession Order.

4.      Return of Child by Sole Managing Conservator—Parent A is ORDERED to return the child to Parent B, if Parent B is entitled to possession of the child, at the end of each of Sole Managing Conservator's exclusive periods of possession, at the place designated in this Standard Possession Order.

5.      Personal Effects—Each conservator is ORDERED to return with the child the personal effects that the child brought at the beginning of the period of possession.

6.      Designation of Competent Adult—Each conservator may designate any competent adult to pick up and return the child, as applicable. IT IS ORDERED that a conservator or a designated competent adult be present when the child is picked up or returned.

7.      Inability to Exercise Possession—Each conservator is ORDERED to give notice to the person in possession of the child on each occasion that the conservator will be unable to exercise that conservator's right of possession for any specified period.

8.      Written Notice—Written notice shall be deemed to have been timely made if received or postmarked before or at the time that notice is due.

[If alternate possession times are used for ending any period of possession (Texas Family Code 153.317), include the following paragraph.]

9.      Notice to School and Sole Managing Conservator—If Parent B's time of possession of the child ends at the time school resumes and for any reason the child is not or will not be returned to school, Parent B shall immediately notify the school and Parent A that the child will not be or has not been returned to school.

[Include the following if applicable.]

The Court finds that Parent B is currently a member of the armed forces of the state or the United States or is reasonably expected to join those forces. The Court further finds that Parent B has designated [name of designee] as a person who may exercise possession of the child on behalf of Parent B during the period that Parent B is deployed under a military deployment as defined by the Texas Family Code and that the possession is in the best interest of the child.

IT IS THEREFORE ORDERED that during periods of deployment, [name of designee] has the right to possession of the child for the periods and in the manner in which Parent B would be entitled to exercise possession under the provisions of this Standard Possession Order as set out above.

IT IS FURTHER ORDERED that Parent A and [name of designee] are subject to the requirements imposed on a conservator listed above in part (g), General Terms and Conditions, of this Standard Possession Order, with [name of designee] considered, for purposes of those requirements, to be Parent B. [Name of designee] has following duties and right during the period that [name of designee] has possession of the child: the duty of care, control, protection, and reasonable discipline of the child; the duty to provide the child with clothing, food, and shelter; and the right to consent to medical, dental, and surgical treatment during an emergency involving an immediate danger to the health and safety of the child. [Name of designee] is subject to any provision in a court order restricting or prohibiting access to the child by any specified individual.

IT IS ORDERED that after the military deployment is concluded and Parent B returns to Parent B's usual residence, [name of designee]'s right to possession terminates and the rights of all affected parties are governed by the terms of any court order applicable when Parent B is not deployed.

This concludes the Standard Possession Order.

# APPENDIX 8
## How to Locate a Mental Health Professional

You may find a local counselor that specializes in working with individuals or couples while in the midst of divorce by contacting any of the following organizations:

American Counseling Association
(www.counseling.org)

American Psychiatric Association
(www.psych.org)

American Psychological Association
(www.apa.org)

National Association of Social Workers
(www.socialworkers.org)

Texas Counseling Association
(www.txca.org)
(each state has its own counseling association)

# APPENDIX 9
## How to Locate a Collaboratively Trained Professional

The International Academy of Collaborative Professionals
(www.collaborativepractice.com)

Collaborative Law Institute of Texas
(www.collablawtexas.com)
(many states have their own collaborative practice association)

# Melinda Eitzen, JD
## www.d-elaw.com

Melinda Eitzen, recently recognized by D Magazine as one of the "Best Lawyers in Dallas" and one of the "Best Family Law Mediators in Dallas", is an attorney on the forefront of the collaborative law movement in Texas, is a partner in the Dallas-Fort Worth area-based family law practice of Duffee + Eitzen.

Focused on multimillion-dollar divorces, custody modifications, paternity cases, and premarital agreements, Melinda Eitzen is highly experienced in all facets of family law, and well versed in managing high-profile cases. She is the daughter of beloved retired Judge, Merrill Hartman, who was a Dallas District Judge for 22 years on both the Civil bench and Family bench.

Melinda Eitzen has utilized her expertise in the practice of Collaborative Law to pen lectures, articles, and books on the subject including co-authoring "Divorce The Collaborative Way. Is It The Way For You?" and "Considering Divorce? Critical Things You Need to Know.". In addition, she has presented dynamic lectures on many family law issues and the practice of family law. She has received the distinction of being a "Super Lawyer" multiple times by Texas Monthly Magazine (every year from 2003-2006 and every year again from 2009-2017) and one of the "Best Lawyers in Dallas" by D Magazine. Melinda is the recipient of numerous awards, particularly for her pro bono work and for teaching others how to do pro bono work.

Melinda has served as President of the Collin County Bar Association and as a Member of the Board of Directors of Texas Lawyers for Children from 2011-2013, as President of the **Plano Bar Association**, as a chair of the Collaborative Law Alliance of Collin County, Vice President of the Collin County Bar Association, chair of the Good Works Committee of the Collin County Bar Association, director of the Dallas Association of Young Lawyers, director of Texas Young Lawyers Association, and chair of the Family Law Section of the Collin County Bar Association.

Melinda Eitzen has a true passion for helping people through difficult times. She has an exceptional mix of both compassion for her clients and an unyielding toughness on her opponents in the courtroom This unique blend gives her clients someone to talk to and someone they can depend on to protect their interests and get them everything they deserve. Melinda Eitzen is your Dallas Family Attorney. You can contact Melinda by calling 214-416-9010 or by emailing her at **melinda@d-elaw.com**.

# Joanna Jadlow, CPA, CFP®, CDFA™
## www.RGTnet.com

Joanna Jadlow has been serving clients in the fields of accounting, financial planning and wealth management since 2001. She was recently recognized by D Magazine as one of the "Top Wealth Managers & Best Financial Planners in Dallas" for the second time. Joanna is Director of Financial Planning at Robertson, Griege & Thoele, one of the most highly regarded wealth management firms in Dallas and recognized nationally as an industry leader. As an independent and fee-only firm, RGT has been serving clients with the highest standards of integrity, excellence and innovation since 1985.

Joanna has worked with clients, attorneys and mental health professionals in divorce matters since 2008. She helps individuals and couples make educated financial decisions that are in the best interest of themselves and their families. Her work includes serving as a neutral financial professional in collaborative divorce cases, as well as working with one spouse in litigated and non-collaborative matters.

In the area of wealth management, Joanna works exclusively with affluent individuals and families managing all aspects of their financial world. She helps clients with complicated financial lives make decisions that support their long-term financial security. She is especially skilled in working with clients who are relatively new to managing wealth and may feel overwhelmed and intimidated. She has expertise in all areas of financial planning, including retirement, estate/gift, risk management, tax, budgeting and investments.

Joanna has been recognized by Dallas Business Journal's 40 Under Forty, D Magazine's Best Financial Planners, Lakewood Service League's Service Hero Award, and Oklahoma Society of CPAs Gold Medal on the CPA Exam. She has been a speaker at various venues including the Sports Lawyers Association and Sports Financial Advisors Association national conferences, as well as for various local groups. Joanna has been quoted in the Dallas Morning News and Kiplinger's Retirement Report. With her passion for service, Joanna also has been involved in many community and professional organizations.

Joanna knows how difficult divorce can be and how hard it is to transition financially from one household to two. She believes in the importance of educating oneself and utilizing a strong team of professionals to get through the process with the best possible outcome.

# Brenda Lee Roberts, M. Ed., LPC
## www.BrendaLeeRoberts.com

Brenda Lee Roberts has been a Licensed Professional Counselor since 2004. She has private practices in Texas and Virginia and focuses her time and energy on helping parents, in the midst of divorce, be the best parents they can be by learning new ways of communicating, creating practical parenting plans, supporting them through the difficult process of informing the children about the divorce and the transition of the children between their two homes.

Prior to her work on collaborative teams, she worked as a court appointed private social study investigator in contested custody cases and as a private home study investigator for adoptions. Brenda has worked with attorneys and financial planners in the collaborative divorce process since 2007. She has participated in many cases and has utilized her experience and expertise to help collaborative teams, spouses and parents. In addition, she has taught "Children in the Middle" classes to parents in the midst of litigated divorces and advanced trainings to Mental Health Professionals working with collaborative teams. She has committed her time to serving on committees and boards that work with families in transition. In addition, she also had the pleasure of participating as a case facilitator/MHP on one of the first CPS Collaborative cases in the nation.

Brenda is a member of the International Academy of Collaborative Professionals, Virginia Collaborative Professionals, Collaborative Law Institute of Texas, the American Counseling Association, Virginia Counseling Association, Texas Counseling Association and Association of Family and Conciliation Courts. She currently serves on the International Academy of Collaborative Professionals Access to Collaboration Task Force that is working to assist professionals in making collaborative divorce accessible to lower income families, Virginia Collaborative Professionals Member At Large Committee and Collaborative Professionals of Richmond Virginia Pro Bono and Marketing Committees.

Brenda's passion has always been to make a difference in how families transition through divorce. It is her belief that co-parents who consistently bring their children's best interests into focus instead of their conflict contribute to their children's futures in immeasurable ways.